WITHDRAWN

America's Paradise Lost

Books by Willard Price:

AMERICA'S PARADISE LOST

RIVERS I HAVE KNOWN

THE AMAZING MISSISSIPPI

INCREDIBLE AFRICA

ROAMING BRITAIN

ADVENTURES IN PARADISE

JOURNEY BY JUNK

THE AMAZING AMAZON

I CANNOT REST FROM TRAVEL

ROVING SOUTH

KEY TO JAPAN

JAPAN AND THE SON OF HEAVEN

JAPAN'S ISLANDS OF MYSTERY

JAPAN RIDES THE TIGER

BARBARIAN

CHILDREN OF THE RISING SUN

PACIFIC ADVENTURE

ANCIENT PEOPLES AT NEW TASKS

THE NEGRO AROUND THE WORLD

AMERICA'S INFLUENCE IN THE ORIENT

For Boys:

SAFARI ADVENTURE

ELEPHANT ADVENTURE

AFRICAN ADVENTURE

WHALE ADVENTURE

VOLCANO ADVENTURE

UNDERWATER ADVENTURE

SOUTH SEA ADVENTURE

AMAZON ADVENTURE

WILLARD PRICE

America's
Paradise Lost

ILLUSTRATED

The John Day Company   New York

To the Hicom and Distads of the Trust Territory of the Pacific Islands who are doing a job against odds

Contents

Marianas

Saipan

Wak[e]

Philippines

GUAM

MICRONESI[A]

Yap

Truk

Palau

Ponape

Sonsorol

Nukuo[ro]

OK[...]

Equator

Hawaii

Kusaie

Marshalls

ingamarangi

Gilberts
(British)

America's Paradise Lost

Hidden Heaven

CONGRESSMAN X was flagged down by a newsman on the steps of the Capitol.

"What are you going to do about Micronesia?" inquired the reporter.

"Mike who?" said Mr. X.

The White House, disturbed by reports of the shameful neglect of America's colony in the Pacific, had urged that Congress do something about it.

The request, one of hundreds, escaped the attention of many solons and bewildered others.

What was this neglected island possession in the far Pacific? Was it Okinawa? Was it Formosa? There had been some mention of "Micronesia," but who ever heard of that?

"What is Micronesia?"

The question was asked in a college quiz program. The college boys did little better than the congressman.

"A disease like amnesia," ventured one contestant.

"Something to do with microscopes," guessed another.

Such unawareness was not surprising. A heavy blanket of secrecy has covered America's world in the Western Pacific. There were two reasons for secrecy.

First, security—the islands are a military base.

Second, colonialism. America is not anxious to be known as a colonial power. And Micronesia is to all intents and purposes a colony, officially known as the Trust Territory of the Pacific Islands.

ℰ

How did it come under the Stars and Stripes?

When Japan attacked Pearl Harbor December 7, 1941, an angry American military commentator declared the war would be over in two weeks. How could puny Japan resist the might of the United States?

He reckoned without Micronesia. That vast barricade of two thousand islands blocked the way to Tokyo. Instead of two weeks, it took four years to force a passage through this formidable barrier to the shores of Japan.

Japan had taken the islands from the Germans in World War I. At the close of the war, the Versailles Conference, at Japan's insistence, assigned the islands to Japan as a "mandate." This meant that the islands remained theoretically the property of the League of Nations, but Japan was authorized to administer them on condition that she should not fortify them and would at all times allow foreigners and foreign ships free access to the group.

Japan defiantly proceeded to fortify the islands, and strictly barred access of non-Japanese personnel and vessels.

Possession of the archipelago fired the war dreams of Japanese militarists. They had long urged the "Southward Advance." It had now been made possible. Micronesia extended the Japanese arm to the equator. Just beyond were the tempting lands of the world's second largest island, New Guinea, countless smaller islands, and the sparsely populated continent of Australia.

On the west the mandate hugged the Philippines, and on the east it elbowed Hawaii.

"These islands are made to order for Japan," declared Admiral Suetsugu.

As war neared and rhetoric waxed, the islands were sloganized as Japan's "lifeline to the south" and Japan's "first line of defense." Behind this line of defense, Japan attacked China. America could bluster in vain. She was shut off from the scene of conflict by an island breakwater which, together with the Japanese home islands, barricaded the entire front of the Asiatic continent against interference from the West.

On the fateful day, Pearl Harbor was attacked from the nearest Micronesian islands, the Marshall group. At the same time the islands farthest west, the Carolines, were the launching pad for an assault upon the Philippines.

After four years of bitter fighting and disastrous loss of men and ships, Japan's surrender was accepted on board the *Missouri* in Tokyo Harbor.

Now it was America's turn to demand suzerainty over the fateful islands. They were invaluable to her and to the Western world, if the future ambitions of both Japan and China were to be held in check.

She was not content to receive them on the old terms of non-fortification and free access. She frankly meant to fortify them when and if necessary, and to bar snooping investigators. In short, she wanted authority to do legally exactly what the Japanese had done illegally.

So the islands were assigned to the United States as a "strategic trusteeship," the only such on earth, the word "strategic" signifying that, unlike all other trusteeships of the United Nations, this one might be closed to visitors and utilized as a military base.

It was so ordered. The islanders themselves were not consulted. Nor did they have any part in determining the form of government under which they would live. The islands became in effect a colony of the United States.

That was just before the great powers became self-conscious about captive peoples and began getting rid of their colonies as rapidly as possible.

Since 1950, no less than 43 colonies have become independent nations!*

Those possessions euphemistically known as "Trust Territories" have all but disappeared from the face of the earth. In 1947 there were eleven such territories. Now only three remain —Nauru and New Guinea, administered, with increasing embarrassment, by Australia; and Micronesia, ward of the United States.

America, traditional champion of independence, finds itself in the acutely uncomfortable position of holding one of the last remaining colonies on earth—and, what is worse, neglecting it shamefully. Naturally, Washington has not cared to publicize the matter. But the UN inspection missions visiting the Trust have been critical. President Kennedy quietly prodded Congress to take action, but without much result; the congressman

* The 43 are Algeria, Burundi, Cambodia, Cameroon, Central African Republic, Chad, Congo (Brazzaville), Congo (Leopoldville), Cyprus, Dahomey, Gabon, Ghana, Guinea, Ivory Coast, Jamaica, Kenya, Kuwait, Laos, Libya, Malagasy, Malaysia, Mali, Malta, Mauritania, Morocco, Niger, Nigeria, Pakistan, Rwanda, Senegal, Sierra Leone, Somalia, Sudan, Tanganyika, Togo, Trinidad, Tunisia, Uganda, Vietnam (North), Vietnam (South), Upper Volta, Western Samoa, Zanzibar.

from Maine or Kansas refused to get excited over islands eight thousand miles from his own constituency.

Congress finally responded in 1962 with a doubled appropriation for the islands. This would seem on the face of it to be a most generous response. Upon analysis, it is not munificent. For ten years the annual appropriation had stood still at less than $8,000,000. In the meantime, costs of all sorts had more than doubled. Rising costs and a nonrising budget meant just one thing: retrogression. From year to year, less could be accomplished. As one Trust official put it, "All activities have registered a *decrease,* due to a restricted total budget."

The doubling of the appropriation has now boosted the Trust economy to what it was ten years before. But the moment of congratulation is brief. With a once-more standstill appropriation, the retrogression from year to year is resumed.

One of President Kennedy's demands, however, is beginning to bear fruit. He urged that the pall of secrecy be lifted and tourists admitted to the islands. Also, businessmen, formerly barred, should be allowed to enter and initiate much-needed industrial enterprises. By throwing the islands open to the public he hoped that "these actions I have taken will foster responsible political development, stimulate new economic activity, and enable the people of the islands to participate fully in the world of today."

These directives have been put into effect by the energetic new High Commissioner of the Trust, M. W. Goding. It is not an overnight job—so drastic a change of policy takes time to implement. Most travelers and even travel agents remain unaware that the previously closed and locked territory is now open. And the islands are not yet prepared to receive a flood of visitors. Transportation must first be improved, and accommodations provided. But a definite start is being made. Mr. Goding informs this writer:

"U.S. citizen travel throughout the Trust Territory is a fact today in Micronesia. The first solid efforts to develop the tourism potential of the Palau District have been undertaken by the Palau Travel Bureau which is centering its efforts around the annual Palau Fair May 22. I have agreed to the charter of our DC-4 provided a maximum and minimum number of tourists make firm commitments for the trip. Limited transportation and housing accommodations have restricted this development in past years, but this is no longer true. Saipan is presently enjoying an increase in the number of visitors who are making full use of the increased air transportation facilities. Members of the Saipan business community have recognized this development potential and are planning better accommodations to attract still greater numbers of visitors."

Now you are welcome not only on the headquarters island, Saipan, but you may visit other islands *if* you can book transportation and accommodation. This is still difficult, but not impossible. Inter-island planes and boats are few, and hotels, though they do exist on all main islands, need to be notified of your coming well in advance.

But almost any inconvenience will be cheerfully tolerated by adventurous wanderers who are willing to trade the jet-plane accessibility of Hawaii and Tahiti for the secluded beauty of the loveliest and least-known atolls of the Pacific. Here is a new world, ripe for the picking.

ᥰ

A vast world. The Trust's two thousand islands are scattered over a sea area of three million square miles—the equivalent of continental United States. It turns into an American lake all of the Pacific from Hawaii to Formosa and from Japan to the equator.

Micronesia means "Sea of Small Islands." It is one of the

three great divisions of the greatest ocean, the others being Polynesia, "Sea of Many Islands," and Melanesia, "Sea of Black Islands." Any one of these seas is three times the size of the Mediterranean.*

Pacific distances are fabulous. The world's greatest ocean occupies more space than all the land on the globe. It would hold two Atlantics and still have room for a few Mediterraneans. Better than half of all the world's water is in the Pacific. Its greatest north-south dimension is 9,300 miles and its greatest width, 10,300. The sun takes ten hours to cross it, nearly half of its circle around the globe. No other ocean plumbs such depths. Its floor is a third deeper on the average than the Atlantic. But there are curious trenches or canyons that drop farther below sea level than the world's highest mountain rises above it. The Mindanao Trench is 37,782 feet deep. Everest is 29,000 feet high.

℘

It is small wonder that in so vast an ocean little Micronesia, extending over a sea only as large as the United States, should have been overlooked.

The islands themselves are so dwarfed by the immensity of the ocean that they appear on a map of the Pacific as mere dots, if at all. And yet some of these dots are of surprising proportions. Palau is 125 miles long. Ponape is a hundred miles around. Truk lagoon is forty miles across. Kwajalein, world's largest coral atoll, was capable of accommodating the entire fleets of the anti-Japanese navies.

The total of two thousand islands is only an approximation —for who can tell how large an island must be to be called an

* Micronesia is made up of four island groups, the Marianas, Carolines, Marshalls, and Gilberts. The Trust Territory includes all except the Gilberts which are British-owned, and the island of Guam acquired by the United States from Spain in 1898.

island? Counting in the islets, the figure is said to stand at 2,-550. The majority are of that highly romantic and romanticized type—the coral atoll, enclosing an iridescent lagoon and studded with islands varying in height from six to 3,166 feet.

Nor is it just the land that is valuable. In this oceanographic age, when the sea around us has assumed new importance; when its depths are probed for minerals and its shallows drilled for oil, when Cousteau has proved by his village on the sea bottom that settlements, even cities, on the floor of the ocean are a distinct possibility in the not far distant future, when overpopulation in many lands is causing increased dependence on aquatic food supplies, when land bases have become vulnerable to nuclear attack and are being replaced by fleets of Polaris-missile submarines which require undersea sanctuary, the vast Micronesian waters are becoming at least as significant as the dots of land.

2.

Paradise Lost

WE had visited the islands in 1935, when they were still under Japanese control. That visit of four months was accomplished with difficulty and danger; certain other observers who went in never came out.

Now we wished to return to compare the American administration with that of the Japanese. Was America doing better or worse than her predecessor?

But when we went to buy tickets we encountered obstacles almost as high as those that had confronted us in Japanese days. The red tape was only slowly being unwound as a result of the President's injunction. Our travel agent was dubious.

"You know, you must have a passport. And do you have a permit from the Department of the Interior? And a Navy permit? And a permit from the High Commissioner of the Trust Territory? And a health certificate, and a police certificate, and a bank certificate, and . . ."

It seemed pretty formidable. With little hope, we wrote letters. One went to Fleet Admiral Chester Nimitz on the chance that he might remember my book, *Japan's Islands of Mystery*, which—merely because it was the only English text available concerning the islands—had been made, upon order of the Admiral, required reading for naval officers in the island war.

He did remember, and smoothed our path to the Chief of Naval Operations in Washington and the High Commissioner of the Trust. Even so, it took four months to obtain all the permissions and papers required. (Future visitors will do better.)

℘

But how simple it was, compared with the year-long tussle we had known in Japan. Located there for five years as a correspondent, I had become fascinated by Japanese stories of the *Nanyo*, as the Japanese called their Micronesian dependency. The word means South Seas.

But when I made application to the proper Japanese government department for permission to visit the Nanyo, I was gently rebuffed.

From 1914, when Japan took the islands, no American journalist had been allowed to step ashore in the Nanyo.

A very few American and British travelers had succeeded in securing passage and had usually been hurried through the archipelago, never permitted to stop over on any island from one boat to the next.

One exception was the British Major Bodley. The Japanese ship on which he was traveling was wrecked on the reef of Yap. Even the ingenious Japanese could think of no way to avoid taking shipwrecked passengers ashore. But he spent only three days on the island before a ship arrived to whisk him away.

Another exception, a pretty grim one, was Colonel Earl Ellis of the United States Marines, who penetrated Palau, looked around, and then died. The Japanese reported that he had drunk himself to death.

Two United States naval officers managed to slip ashore on

Ponape. Nothing more was heard of them until Japan informed the United States that they had lost their lives in an unfortunate accident. A request that the bodies be returned to the United States was refused.

Major Bodley, bitter over Japanese refusal to let him see any island except for as long as the ship lay in port, wrote me in 1935:

> Unless you have strings which you can pull with strength, I think you will find difficulties in getting a passage—much less stopovers.

After years in Japan, I had strings, but pulling them seemed to avail nothing.

More successful was Alexander Hume Ford, Director of the Pan Pacific Union. Because of the hands-across-the-seas nature of his organization, he was accredited with being a "true friend" of Japan and was allowed a through ticket.

Upon his return, I met him in the place where one always meets anyone—the lobby of Tokyo's Imperial Hotel.

The captain of the Japanese ship on which he had traveled had been very cooperative, he told me, and had given him much information about the islands.

"But did you get off the ship and stay in the islands?"

He looked at me with some alarm.

"My dear man," he said, "that isn't done."

I wrote to Ernst Lang, head of the Liebenzeller Mission which supervised some German missionaries left over from the German regime. He replied warily, not knowing whether he dared have anything to do with me.

> The Japanese who are now in possession of the islands are very suspicious, therefore you must not be surprised if they examine you and observe wherever you go. They are doing so with every foreigner. For that reason we do not like to have much connection with foreigners visiting the islands, but if

you are going as missionaries, that will be another thing, I hope.

We could not pretend to be going as missionaries, therefore had to bear up under the suspicion that we were going as spies.

Foreigners could not be absolutely barred, because the mandate stipulated free access to the islands. But they could be, and were, artfully discouraged.

"Full up" was the first excuse of the Tokyo steamship office. When I insisted upon seeing the passenger list and found that the ship was anything but full up, there were other excuses.

It was a very dangerous voyage, I was told, the shipping lanes were full of treacherous reefs, typhoons were frequent, tropical diseases were prevalent, and the natives were savage headhunters.

Moreover the ships, all being Japanese, served nothing but Japanese food. My wife and I might grow weary of rice, bean curd, raw fish, and octopus tentacles.

And there was no place to stay on the islands. There were no hotels.

"We can live in Japanese inns."

"On most islands there are none."

"We have an 'Explorer's Tent.' It can be set up under any palm tree."

"But each piece of land belongs to some native."

"Perhaps he will rent it. Or take us into his house. He may be glad to have paying guests."

The passenger agent looked pained.

"Live with the natives!"

"Why not?" And I tried to make clear how valuable such contacts would be for the purpose of securing certain ethnological material wanted by the National Geographic Society and the American Museum of Natural History.

But considerate officialdom continued to be solicitous of our comfort. And suspicious of our motives.

An officer of the *Kempeitai*, Japanese gestapo, came to our house in Hayama. He had a notebook. He smilingly asked our ages, our fathers' names, mothers' names, grandfathers' names, grandmothers' names, names of all places we had ever lived in or visited. Finally he asked:

"What do you wish to see in the islands?"

I could hardly say "Fortifications." So I shrugged it off with "Fauna and flora."

He wrote that down. Then he asked, "Are they friends of yours?"

Amused, I answered, "Yes."

"How old are they?"

"Well, Fauna may be ten million years old, and Flora considerably older."

It was not prudent to joke with the Kempeitai. Mrs. Price unknowingly saved the situation by coming in at that moment from the kitchen with a plate of hot American doughnuts. The officer put away his notebook.

For months we were put off with objections and excuses.

Meanwhile, in Geneva, the Mandates Commission was asking very pointed questions. Why, they inquired of Japan's representative, had an American ship of scientists bent on viewing an eclipse of the sun been refused entry to mandate waters? Why were foreign ships not allowed in the harbors? Why were the island airports not accessible to all nations?

The Commission knew of my attempts, and the attempts of others in the past, to enter the forbidden islands. They charged

Japan with barring foreigners. Japan's delegate at Geneva heatedly denied that foreigners were barred. The controversy was published in the European and American press. The discussion was doing Japan no good.

One morning when the cables were particularly hot with criticism of Nippon for her suspected militarization of the mandate, I was received with smiles at the government South Seas Bureau. Tickets for my wife and myself were pressed into my hands.

"Japan is being unjustly accused," the official said. "We have decided that you should go and see for yourself."

I paid for the tickets and demanded a paper authorizing us to land on any island and go where we pleased. Grudgingly, it was provided.

Our troubles were over.

But I soon found that the document was worthless. The Japanese captains of the ships on which we traveled had instructions to prevent us from leaving the ship at any port.

Our troubles had only begun.

This time it was comparatively easy. Pockets abulge with documents, we jetted to Hawaii and on to Guam. Thence, a small prop plane skips to Saipan, headquarters of the Trust Territory.

Saipan as the beauty-conscious tourist sees it, is a paradise. As the sociologist or economist sees it, it is something less.

The island is fourteen miles long and five wide. It is a delightful semi-atoll. The entire west shore is flanked by a lagoon protected by a coral reef. The island surface is vivid green and gently rolling, the highest point being Mount Tapotchau, 1,554 feet.

The soft-as-butter air reminds us that we are only fifteen de-

grees from the equator. To the visitor from chillier climes the
scene is exciting and exotic, a tropic fairyland of coconut palms,
breadfruit, banana, flame trees, and tree ferns. The oleander
and scarlet hibiscus spread riots of color. Also flowering gor-
geously is the crepe myrtle called by the Japanese *sarusuberi*

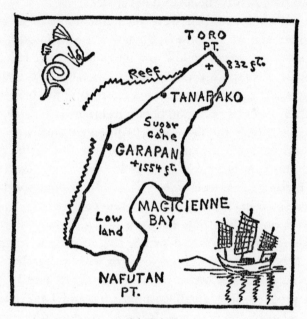

SAIPAN

(monkey slide) because the trunk is so slippery that a monkey
cannot climb it. There are also odd "sleeping plants" which
close their leaves at sunset and open them at sunrise. They are
indeed so sensitive to light that they will fold when a dark
cloud obscures the sun and open when it passes. We recognize
the small tree known to science as the *Barringtonia asiatica,* the
poisonous fruit of which is crushed and dropped into pools. It
has a narcotic effect upon the fish which, stupefied, float belly-
up to the surface and are readily scooped in with a hand net.

The poison does not affect the edibility of the fish.

Fruit is abundant. We sample papayas, bananas, custard apples, and guavas. The most delicious fruit is not yet ripe— the mango. The tree on which it grows is one of nature's most magnificent, with a glossy broad head casting so dense a shade that "sleeping plants" beneath it never wake.

The male rose-crowned fruit dove announces to us with its loud colors that we are now in the latitude of tropical birds. Its colors are rose, green, yellow, orange, and purple. How could any female of its species resist it when it perches in the sunlight, presses its bill against its breast while erecting the bright feathers at the back of its neck, and booms its low call?

A comic bird is the megapode flying as sluggishly as a cargo plane and waddling when it walks. It is useful in the garden, for it industriously scrapes up the decayed leaves and rubbish into a mound where it lays its eggs. It is half domesticated and will come running if you knock two stones together.

A black object flies close over our heads, flapping slowly like a crow, and an unpleasant odor like that of dirty wet rags floats down. A boy brings the thing to earth with a slingshot. It is a flying fox, three feet broad from tip to tip. Its face is foxlike, with a pinched nose, small pointed ears, and large eyes. The flesh is eaten by the islanders. It is said to be good though a bit tough, and has no odor after the skin is removed. We don't try it.

The people of the island are the gentle Chamorros. They have been here so long that no one knows whence they came. Spain once ruled the Marianas, and Tagalogs from the Spanish Philippines came to these islands and intermarried with the Chamorros—and the Spaniards added their quota. The Chamorros of today are a blend of three lively races. Their color is light, their language is half Spanish, their women wear the long skirts and balloon sleeves of the Philippines, and their men play guitars.

On our previous visit we had stayed at the balconied, tropical-Spanish hacienda of Concepción Reyes. The home of this handsome widow was always overflowing with relatives, friends, and perfect strangers, for if you hear the sound of music in a Chamorro house, you just walk in.

Music there was, day and night, and dancing on the floor of polished wood—bouncing dances that made the colored pictures of saints and angels tremble on the walls. But not on Sundays. Then guitars were laid aside, the men put on embroidered coats, the women placed high combs in their hair and mantillas over their shoulders, and all went to the Spanish mission.

Now there is an inn, the Saipan Hotel, boasting thirty-nine rooms, a good dining room, and dancing nearly every night. And the island, locked and barred against tourists for fifty years, now invites them with the slogan, SAIPAN: GATEWAY TO MICRONESIAN BEAUTY.

That's all very well. But what do the islanders think of it?

🙚

An eighty-five-year-old Chamorro chief when asked, "Are your people happy under American administration?" replied gently:

"That doesn't matter. We take what comes."

Complimented on his good English, he said, "It's fortunate that we pick up languages easily. I can remember when Spain ruled these islands, we had to speak Spanish, or be flogged. That ended in 1899. Then for fifteen years we had to use German. For thirty years after that nothing would do but Japanese. And now we are expected to speak English."

He sat nodding to himself for a few moments. Then he added with a wry smile, "I hope we don't have to learn Russian."

It typified the life of the Micronesian. He has never been asked what he wanted since the first white intruders landed on his islands.

"What were the Spanish like?"

"They never bothered us much."

"And the Germans?"

"They were very strict."

"The Japanese?"

"They did a lot. But they didn't do it for us. They did it for themselves. There were too many people in Japan—they had to go somewhere. More than a hundred thousand of them came to the islands. They made their homes here. They started a lot of industries. They needed workers, and they saw us. We didn't want to work for them, but we had to, or their police would punish us. Perhaps it was good for us. The pay was poor, but it was more money than we had ever had. Every man was rich. Then the war—and the Americans."

"And how has it been with the Americans?"

"Ah so, the Americans." The chief hesitated. "I don't know what to say. At first it was good. Your Navy was boss in Saipan. Your Navy has much money. We worked for the Navy. Three out of every four worked for the Navy. With the pay we bought radios, and some of us even had—what you call—flush toilets. Every family had a car. Perhaps it was an old Army jeep, but it was a car. Then in 1962 there was a change. The Navy wasn't boss any more. Then it was bad."

Why it turned bad requires some explanation.

After the war the Department of the Interior was charged

with the administration of all the Trust islands—except Saipan. That was placed under Navy control because of its special value as a military base. Nearest of the islands to Japan, it had been the launching pad for attacks upon Japanese cities. It and Okinawa were and are in a position to patrol the entire coastline of Asia from Vladivostok to Saigon.

But with some lessening of strain in the Far East, and repeated proddings from the UN which wanted to know why the U.S. military still held territory seized after the war, the Navy finally yielded control of Saipan to the Department of the Interior.

This was a hard blow for the Saipanese, because the Navy has always enjoyed generous appropriations and Interior has not— particularly when doing an exterior job. And what could be more exterior than the administration of islands on the far side of the world?

So the good pay is ended, the good jobs are gone. Saipan had been living upon a larger grant than all the other islands of the Trust combined. Now it has been trimmed down to size. Its hope of recovery from the devastation of war is dimmed. The wartime destruction of properties was severe. The High Commissioner reported in his *Handbook of Information,* 1964:

> The city of Garapan on Saipan, once a city of over 29,000 people, was reduced to rubble. Saipan has not yet recovered from this devastation and the great majority of people still live in temporary houses built from wartime salvaged materials.

The flush toilets installed during the flush Navy days are already a rarity. At last count, less than two hundred of the 1,257 homes had such facilities. The jeeps are being junked for lack of money to buy gasoline or spare parts.

Perhaps no one is to blame. The Navy can hardly be censured because it treated the people too well. The Department of the Interior is not responsible for lack of funds. Even that congressman from Kansas can be regarded with understanding. He is and should be most concerned with the needs of Kansas. Kansas can re-elect him, Saipan cannot. As one congressman said very candidly, when challenged with the plight of Micronesia, "There are no voters out there."

※

And, anyhow, why can't the islanders simply go back to fish and coconuts? Argued one official, "The best thing we can do for our wards is to leave them alone." Why not let them return to the happy days of old?

It is a bit late for that.

"When I was a boy," said David Ramarui, college graduate, to visiting reporter Don Oberdorfer of the *Post*, "our class used to go to the radio station to sing on the air. We grew up under modern conditions. It's simply nonsense to expect us to go back to living in grass huts under the coconut trees."

The Japanese had already made such a "return to nature" impossible before the United States set foot on Saipan. The island swarmed with Japanese and hummed with activity. The metropolis, Garapan, offered more jobs than Chamorros could fill and was forced to import helpers from Okinawa. Its main street was a close-packed pageant of department stores, specialty shops, small factories, restaurants, theaters, and a half mile of geisha houses.

The harbor was full of large deep-sea fishing boats. Saipan exported fabulous quantities of fish to Japan. Now it is a different story. In 1962, Saipan *imported* $47,000 worth of canned fish.

Saipan's sugar exports came to $6,000,000 annually. The whole island was awave with lush green sugarcane. It was a beautiful sight as we viewed it from the deck of the *Yokohama Maru* in 1935. The ship dropped anchor a half mile out. We eagerly awaited the lighter that would take us ashore.

ॐ

"You won't want to land here." The captain had come up behind us as we stood at the rail.

I reminded him that we had a permit from the Tokyo authorities.

"Ah, so," he said. "But they left it to me to arrange details. I fear you would not be comfortable on this island. There are many flies."

I tried not to smile. You must never be amused at a Japanese if you hope to get around him. And you must agree with him.

"Indeed!" I said gravely. "In that case, we would be much better off on board."

A lighter drawn by a tug came up on the starboard side to take off passengers. The captain was busy on the port side, watching the cargo barges. Just as the tug was beginning to pull the passenger lighter away, we ran down the companionway and hopped in.

There was a shout above us. The captain was glaring down from the bridge. Mary smiled her most engaging smile and held up something she had brought from our cabin. It was a fly swatter.

The captain's face was a study. Never were a smile and a scowl more perfectly combined in one expression.

On the dock was the ubiquitous Japanese policeman.

"You are the Americans, yes?" he accused us. "I heard about you. But I understood you would remain on board."

"So sorry," I said in the best Japanese manner. "Slight mistake."

I produced the paper. He waved it aside.

"I shall have to take you to the governor," he announced sternly.

This was all that could be desired, for the path to the governor's bungalow led for two miles through town and countryside, affording an excellent idea of Saipan. And when the squat, jovial little governor saw us and found us harmless he permitted us to roam at will over his precious island where furtive fortification in preparation for the coming war was already under way.

ᘯ

The captain was right—there were flies on Saipan. A sweet smell not only hung over the roaring sugar mill, but seemed to have attracted all the flies of the Pacific.

In a small wayside fruit shop we had lunch, fighting the flies for every bite. Our Japanese policeman ordered bean soup. When it was set before him it contained six flies. We watched with curiosity. Would he send it back? Would he pick out the flies with his chopsticks?

He raised the bowl to his mouth, locked his long upper teeth over the edge to form a sieve, and drank the soup. The six flies remained in the bowl.

He smiled. "We get used to them," he said.

Now the flies are gone, but so is the sugarcane. Cattle graze on the former cane land. Farms are few—men employed for years in well-paying town jobs don't care to go back to farming. Industries are slow in developing. This is due partly to native inertia, partly to past government policy. The government, very properly, has wanted Micronesian industry to be carried on by and for the Micronesians.

This high-minded policy was reaffirmed by High Commissioner M. W. Goding in 1962:

"Many Micronesians," he noted, "who remember the pre-war days, have a tendency to compare the pre-war economy with that of today. Actually, this comparison is somewhat misleading. Before the war there were more Japanese colonists in the Territory than there were Micronesians. While it might be true that the pre-war economy in comparison was a flourishing one, businesses were owned and operated by the Japanese for the Japanese, with Micronesians receiving in most cases only fringe benefits.

"Our policy," the High Commissioner continued, "has been that the economic development in this area should be by the Micronesians themselves for themselves. Thus, when we compare the pattern of pre-war economy with that of today, we should not count the number of buildings, the number of stores, and the like, but we should remember that a basic difference in philosophy is present. Formerly, there was exploitation of the area for outsiders; today, we want the development to be by and for the people of the Territory."

The "Hicom"—as the High Commissioner is known within the Trust—was simply stating Washington policy. But Washington was even then about to temper that policy. The Kennedy Administration was upset by the 100-page report of the UN touring mission which declared that young Micronesians could not obtain capital to start new ventures. Nor could they get the necessary technical and business training. There was, according to the report, "no coordinated plan for economic development." The economy had "been allowed to remain static for too long."

The President advised a modification of the "Micronesia for the Micronesians" philosophy. If capital was needed, why not let American private capital flow in? If technical training was needed, why not allow American technicians to enter and to start industries which would then employ and train Micronesians?

This is a ticklish business—as the islanders found out during the Japanese regime. Japanese fishing experts flocked south, built deep-sea fishing craft, made a fabulous success out of the previously moribund fishing industry. But did the Micronesians learn deep-sea fishing from the experts? They did not. The executives, the boat builders, the crews, the processors, were all Japanese. Instead of training the islanders, the Japanese deliberately excluded them from all important posts.

It may be that under an administration more concerned with the welfare of the islanders, this pattern will not be repeated. At any rate, the experiment has begun. American capital investment is now admitted. Enterprises by Americans, but not selfishly for Americans, are encouraged.

In the fishing industry, for example, most of the American tuna firms have sent representatives to look over prospects and discuss plans for commercial fishing development. Among the major companies interested are Van Camp, Bumble Bee Tuna, Star Kist, Westgate, Wilbur and Ellis. Other companies have proposed to send representatives in the near future. An extensive Van Camp plant is already operating.

In the meantime, some islanders are getting preliminary training. It may seem odd that people largely dependent upon fish should need training in fishing. But most fishing by islanders has been by small boat in reef-protected waters. They lacked the money to build huge motorized fishing craft and knew nothing of the art of laying a main line twenty to seventy miles long supporting hundreds of hooks that catch fish in shipload lots. Students now being trained at the Fisheries School in Koror and in Hawaii may be able to play an active role in the new fishing industry.

The grim tension of Saipan in pre-war days has yielded to an ambience much more tolerant and relaxed. No longer is it a hotbed of conspiracy and suspicion. A Chamorro may speak his mind about the Hicom and Americans in general.

On our previous visit I had jealously guarded my reputation as an innocent and nonpolitical naturalist. I had turned an apparently blind eye upon the fortification of Magicienne and Tanapako harbors and the mountain of Tapotchau. I even agreed with a young Japanese friend, Toda by name, when he expatiated on Japanese achievements.

"Europeans don't belong here," he said. "They had the Nanyo for three hundred years. We have done more to develop the Nanyo in twenty years than they did in three hundred."

Which could not be denied.

"So long as Japan does not use the islands for military purposes," I suggested, "I'm sure everybody is quite willing that they should be left to Japan to develop."

Toda's face tightened. "It is not for others to dictate Japan's conduct. If the Emperor chooses to use the Nanyo for military purposes, his will supersedes the rules of any League of Nations."

It was a Japanese habit to deride the Chamorro and his Catholic faith. An irritated Chamorro lad had the courage to say to a taunting Japanese, "Please respect our God as we respect your Emperor."

He was thrown in prison and never seen again—for it was the most grave of offenses to speak in the same breath of the Christian God and the Japanese Emperor, direct descendant of the Sun Goddess Amaterasu.

℣

Another who disappeared never to be seen again was Amelia Earhart. It is now believed that after her plane crashed in the

Marshalls she and her navigator, Fred Noonan, were brought to the military headquarters in Saipan and there died.

More than a hundred of the older Saipanese testify to it. It made a deep impression upon them because, as one said, "in 1937 it was unheard of for a woman to be a flier." Among the witnesses are many presumably reliable persons: police investigators, church leaders, military men—Captain Jose Quintanilla and Sergeant Edward Camacho of the Guam Police Department, Saipan law-enforcement officer Sheriff Manual T. Sablan, Sergeant Tony Benavente, attorney Edward Wiles, Dr. Manual Aldon, Jesus P. Boyer of the present Saipan legislature, storekeeper Juan Guerrero Reyes, Francisco Tudela of the insuar constabulary, merchant Jose Pangelinan, Brother Gregario of the Yap Catholic Mission, Jesus Salas who had been imprisoned by the Japanese in the cell next to that of the woman flier. It is said that Miss Earhart and Noonan were condemned as spies; the woman died in prison and Noonan was executed.

The spy phobia of that delicate period was quite natural, and indeed it continued under the administration of U.S. naval officers who did not welcome promiscuous visitors to this vulnerable naval base. Now these tensions have been largely dissipated; but dissipated, too, are the high hopes. Vanished beyond recall is the natural paradise of the age before Magellan reached the Marianas. Gone too is the more recent paradise of plumbing, refrigeration, the hot rod and money in the pocket under the stimulation of the Japanese and the opulence of the American military. Now a disillusioned but remarkably patient people hang in a state of suspended animation, unable to go back to the ancient simplicity, unequipped to go forward.

3

June, Moon, Lagoon

THESE two thousand bits of heaven are such stuff as dreams are made on. And popular music. A sojourn in the sea of atolls should be prescribed as elementary education for anyone who aspires to pen romantic rhymes or pagan love songs. They make a poet of the most soulless clod.

This education, like all good education, is not too easy to get. Once a week a small Grumman Albatross takes off from Saipan on a round of the most important island centers. Once a month a Trust steamer makes the circuit. Planes are booked far ahead with a waiting list of thirty or more, and a booked passenger may be "bumped" at the last moment to make room for an official on some more important errand. As for the hundreds of islands remote from the centers, they are fortunate if visited every two months, six months, or once a year. Service will be stepped up a bit, now that a DC-4 has been added to the fleet.

The Albatross dropped us into a turquoise harbor where a launch waited to take us ashore. After a few weeks the amphibian picked us up again to deposit us in another lagoon. And so on. This much-punctuated journey took us to the fairy atoll of Majuro, the immense lagoon of Kwajalein, the cloud-capped heights of Ponape, the unique lake in the sea known as Truk, Yap, where the Stone Age still defies the age of glass and concrete, and the fabulous 200-island archipelago of Palau. From each center we side-tripped by boat or plane to outlying islands. Each constellation was different from the next, the only common denominator being that all hugged the equator, all were air-conditioned by the trade wind, all were beautiful and all were blessed or cursed by Progress.

Our first and farthest stop was Majuro. From this easternmost point, we would work our way back through the islands to Guam.

The amphibian plane, thanks to the fact that its wings are above the windows, allows us to see down without obstruction into the fascinating labyrinth of the Forbidden Isles. We pass over the coconut and breadfruit forests of Guam, over dramatic, black rocky shores, and away east.

The atolls that appear and disappear beneath are hard to believe. From our vantage point only a mile high, we are far enough away to get a sweeping view of an entire atoll with its ring of coral reef bucking the white surf rolling in from the deep blue sea and its placid sapphire lagoon dotted with white-beached islands—yet we are close enough to see every essential detail, the forests of coconut palms, the thatch huts, the outrigger canoes winging along under lateen sails, the fishermen casting their nets, and the divers for pearl shell among the colorful corals twenty feet down in the incredibly clear water.

But most of the passengers are old hands. They have seen this sort of thing many times. They are Trust employees, and to them all these scenic wonders are an old story. They are reading books.

Now I approve of anyone who reads books. I crane to see what they are reading. Doubtless something relating to their job.

No, not exactly. The Public Works Director is absorbed in a spicy paperback whose cover illustration suggests a compromising situation and bears the title *He Learned the Hard Way*. The reader is not learning about public works.

A German or a Japanese would be deep in a technical study connected with his profession. Behind the paperback reader is Catholic Bishop Kennally who is boning up on his job—reading the Bible and Catholic journals—and that is doubtless how he became a bishop, and is one reason why the Catholic church is becoming dominant in the islands.

Not that we mean to censure the paperback reader. Public works is a dull subject and the official in charge of it needs a little relaxation.

Across the aisle from these gentlemen, a Trust official is deep in a book on Hong Kong. Trust people are much traveled. Interest in travel is a big factor in bringing them here. Not that they mind benefiting their fellow man—but they could do that at home.

Their contract with the Trust is for two years. Then they have two and a half or three months' vacation, and many use it for travel.

This man across the aisle, Staff Anthropologist DeYoung, has been to Angkor Wat seven times. In a few days now he must go to New York to report to the UN—and he will come back the long way, around the world, short-way fare paid by the Trust Territory and he paying the difference.

We have known Mr. DeYoung long enough to realize his complete devotion to his work. And every anthropologist should take a keen interest in the ways of people everywhere. But we shall come upon some officials who do not have the same watertight excuse for their extracurricular interests.

A jet is as silent as the tomb compared with this gristmill. In a small amphibian the engines are close together overhead, so it sounds as if the roof would fall in at any moment. Only mouth-to-ear conversation is possible.

Many times we thump violently through stormy clouds, but susceptible passengers have been thoroughly Dramamined and don't mind it.

An emergency brings us down on Truk lagoon. One of the two engines has conked out. Certain spare parts are needed. The co-pilot is dispatched to the warehouse of the Truk Trading Company to get them.

He comes back empty-handed. The parts are not available. A radiogram could be sent to Saipan and the items would come on the plane next week.

"To hell with that," says the pilot and stalks off to the nearest village. There he collects some hairpins and clothespins. With these, plus considerable ingenuity, he patches the engine and we go on our way.

❦

We flew on over more incredible atolls to Majuro, seat of the administration of the Marshall Islands District.

We were met by the District Administrator (commonly and quite respectfully called the Distad) and were housed in a guest house within thirty feet of the ever-rolling surf coming in on the trade wind from the east.

It was a true South Sea island setting. The air was as soft as silk. The coconut palms leaned in the breeze. Their golden-yellow nuts full of nourishing food and cool drink dropped one by one to earth with a heavy plunk. The breadfruit trees, pandanus, papayas and mangoes bent under the weight of ripening fruit.

It was only a few hundred feet from the ocean shore with its restless waves to the lagoon shore on which the water lay as still as glass.

Our house was very oddly windowed to keep out the spray. The windows were horizontal instead of vertical. Try to imagine that.

It worked. The wind could not blow directly into the room. It struck the wall and its burden of spray ran down to the ground. Some of the air, with its force broken, was deflected upward through the window where it struck a baffle which turned it into the room. So the room was ventilated, but not blown to pieces.

The wind might blow till it burst its cheeks, the spray fly, the tropical rain pour, and through the always-open windows not one drop came in.

The only drawback was that the house was as blind as a bat. You could see nothing through the windows, except the ground. To enjoy the view you had to step outdoors. This was usually well worth while. Storms were infrequent. The trade wind was usually gentle and refreshingly cool although this was summer and Majuro lies within seven degrees of the equator.

4

Atolls of Sunrise and Sunset

MAJURO lagoon is twenty miles long and from three to five miles wide. Along the encircling reef are strung some twenty charming islands lushly clothed in tropical foliage. The chief of these islands is Majuro itself, headquarters of the District Administration for all the Marshalls.

The fifteen thousand Marshallese inhabit a fling of islands so extensive that no District Administrator has ever been able to get around to all of them, or ever will. The 1,150 islands are scattered over an ocean area of 180,000 square miles. The islands lie in two roughly parallel columns. The eastern column is imaginatively called the Ratak (Sunrise) Chain, and the western, the Ralik (Sunset) Chain.

How to keep in touch with the people of more than a thousand islands that spatter a sea eight hundred miles from north to south and seven hundred wide is an unsolved puzzle. The government's *Handbook of Information* comments defensively: "The problem of transportation and logistics is apparent when the enormous geographic spread and the physical isolation of the more remote atolls is considered."

The inhabitants of a remote island must do for themselves.

They are in a world alone. They are close, sometimes uncomfortably close, to the eternal sea. Nowhere does the land rise more than thirty-three feet above sea level. During severe storms the lower islands are entirely inundated by the waves. The people clamber into the coconut palms while the sea roars beneath them. Sometimes houses, palms, people, and all else are swept away.

Any volcanic islands which the reefs may once have encircled have long since been submerged or worn away, and nothing remains within the atoll but a calm lagoon. The reef at some points is narrow; at others it widens to form an island. The islands, being low, are not easily detected by exploring ships. Even today, vessels sail by them unaware of their existence.

The Marshalls were discovered by the Spaniard de Saavedra in the sixteenth century. Because the natives were picturesquely tattooed he called the islands Los Pintados, "The Painted Ones." English captains later visited the islands and they were named after Captain Marshall, who explored them in 1788. He hoped to see them added to the British Empire. But the British government was not interested.

The Russians however were interested—and might be again. The first close examination of the islands was made by Lieutenant Kotzebue of the Russian Navy, in 1817 and 1824. He made the first hydrographic reports of the islands and wrote detailed descriptions of the people, plants and animals. A few years later the Russian Chramschenko made more studies, and he was followed by Shantz, a member of the Russian Navy, in 1835.

Russia might have capped off exploration with possession if she could have foreseen that such islands as Bikini and Eniwetok would some day become invaluable nuclear testing sites and Kwajalein a great missile base. But such matters were undreamed of, and the islands seemed very far away.

Spain was their nominal master for three hundred years, then sold them to Germany. Japan picked them up in 1914, lost them in 1944. Then it was America's turn.

Actually it was a return, for Americans had been here long before. The early American record is not one to be proud of. Syphilis and tuberculosis were the gifts of the whalers. They made drunken murderous forays upon the natives. American ships became most unwelcome and many were destroyed by the angry islanders. Innocent crews suffered along with the guilty. An unoffending captain was picked up bodily by a great chief and his brains dashed out against a rock. Sailors were decapitated.

Then the ship named *Morning Star* arrived. It was a beautiful sailing clipper, but with auxiliary steam. The captain called for canoes to tow the ship into the lagoon against the strong tide. The natives dutifully performed this service, craftily planning to destroy the ship and kill all on board. But the king intervened just in time. He had heard of the *Morning Star*—it was a ship of mercy paid for by the pennies of Boston children, and its passengers were the first missionaries to the Marshalls. That was in 1857.

The missionary, whether he intends to do so or not, always opens the way for trade, and it was not long before American trading ships were making regular calls at the Marshalls. The business methods of these trading buccaneers were often more shrewd than honest.

"He businessed me," became a current saying among natives, meaning, "He cheated me." And since American whalers and traders were always fighting, an islander threatening another would think it appropriate to say, "I'll Merikan you!"

The traders came to the brisk little American missionary, Miss Hoppin: "Don't let them use those words that way. It's an insult to our business and to Americans."

"Why don't *you* stop them?"

"They mind you. They won't mind us. How could we stop them?"

"By changing your business methods," suggested Miss Hoppin. She took the sting out of it by placing before them a bowl of hot candied bananas baked in coconut milk.

The net result of early American influence upon the Marshalls was more favorable than we would have a right to expect. When we visited Micronesia during the Japanese regime, a Japanese official complained to me, "The Marshalls people can't get their minds off America. They call it their adopted country."

The Governor of Jaluit said, "Until we can stop American mission education and replace it with Japanese education, we can never turn the natives our way."

And an island chief commented, "When the Japanese don't treat us right we go to the Americans. They talk with the Japanese and fix things up."

Small wonder that no more Americans were allowed to come in, and those already in were finally expelled.

The Japanese, left to themselves, failed to win the love of the islanders, and the people of this great archipelago next door to Hawaii hoped vaguely for the day when, like the Hawaiians, they might come into closer association with the United States.

❦

Curiously enough, there has never been any direct communication between Hawaii and the Marshalls. Hawaii looked eastward. The Marshallese looked westward, for it was from the west that their overlords came—the Spaniards, the Germans, the Japanese. They still look to the west because their government emanates from Saipan, located at the extreme western edge of Micronesia, and their supplies, if any, come from the same source.

You feel very far away in Majuro. You are at the end of the line. No other Trust islands are so far from the home base at Saipan. Cargo ships from the outside world call at Saipan or Guam, are unloaded, and the goods are warehoused for weeks or months until room can be found for them on a small Trust steamer bound for the islands. This vessel goes everywhere before coming here. Majuro is the last stop.

The consequence is that the eggs we have for breakfast are three months old and can stand alone. Christmas cards not air-mailed arrive for Easter.

The well-managed native-owned Marshalls Import-Export Company in Majuro (the firm is commonly called Mieco) orders butter from Australia. It arrives three months later. Flour from the same source takes six months. Evaporated milk is received from Holland in six months. Corned beef from Argentina comes through in seven months, if all goes well, and is on sale at once in the Mieco store in Majuro.

But that is fast service. Delivery is not so prompt in the outlying islands. Every two or three months the *Mieco Queen,* owned by the company, takes on a stock of goods and sets sail for the far islands. She pauses near the most populous atolls, ignoring the rest, and eager customers come off in outrigger canoes to visit the floating store and restock their larders.

This isolation is not altogether a bad thing. On Majuro itself many people live under slum conditions in shacks made of scraps of rusty iron. On the outlying islands we visited living conditions were more primitive but more pleasant. Cool thatch had not given way to hot and unsightly scrap iron. The people did not depend upon government handouts but relied upon their own resources. They ate, not from cans, but from the produce of their own trees and taro patches.

"We like being let alone," said one island chief. And we were later to meet a chief who had requested permission to settle some of his people on the remote and uninhabited island of Oroluk. The astonished Distad objected:

"But our ships wouldn't be able to get there more than two or three times a year."

"That's all right," replied the chief happily.

That was exactly what he and his people wanted—to be alone. He proposed to begin with a community of ten persons. Already he had more than a hundred applicants for the privilege of being one of the favored ten. We flew over Oroluk. It consisted of a long wavering line of reef encompassing a large lagoon and on the reef lay one green island. Surely there was no place on earth where ten people could be more alone.

However, there's another side to the picture. It is well to be shielded from some of the blasting heat of civilization, but there's no advantage in disease and mental stagnation. The recluses on far islands suffer for lack of modern medicines, schoolbooks, simple machines, improved methods of agriculture.

5

Mother Hubbard to Bikini

AS we lay on the sand beach before our little blind house, there was a rustling in the bushes and a woman emerged. She was concealed from head to toe in a voluminous mother hubbard—the nightgownlike garment prescribed by missionaries many years ago to hide the disgraceful human form.

She made straight for the water. Without so much as lifting the hem of her garment, she waded in. She proceeded until only her head remained above the surface.

"I hope she doesn't try to swim in that thing," Mary said anxiously.

She didn't. She merely splashed about, then rubbed herself rather ineffectively through the fabric, came out, and sat on the sand to dry. The brisk sea breeze penetrating her dripping gown made her shiver.

We had no sooner reflected on the part played by clothing in vastly increasing the incidence of tuberculosis, pneumonia, and other respiratory and skin diseases among people accustomed to nudity, than the answer came tripping out of the bushes. The answer was a pretty Micronesian lass clad in the briefest of bikinis.

She plunged in, swam the crawl, the backstroke, the spiral, came out for a drip-dry run on the beach, and disappeared.

It typified the old and new in the Marshalls.

The advent of the bikini should not have surprised us, for its very creation was inspired in these islands.

You will look in vain for the bathing-suit term "bikini" in any dictionary older than 1946. The nuclear explosions of that year on the island of Bikini prompted a bathing-suit designer to create something guaranteed to produce an equivalent shock. The 1964 Webster's defines a bikini as derived "from Bikini, atoll of the Marshall Islands, site of the atomic bomb tests of 1946; from the comparison of the effects wrought by a scantily clad woman to the effects of an atomic bomb."

The bikini is no longer atomic. Even the missionary is more shockproof than he used to be. He is less insistent that Pacific islanders should become Bostonians overnight. Perhaps they will do very well as Pacific islanders.

Finally convinced by the doctors, some missionaries acknowledge that a brown skin can be healthier, cleaner, and more handsome than a stained nightgown or ragged shirt and trousers. Traditional dances, previously banned, are now tolerated and sometimes even encouraged. The natural gaiety of the Micronesian may not be a bad thing after all. Perhaps it is even a virtue. Sexual promiscuity before marriage is deplored; but it must be acknowledged that Marshallese faithfulness after marriage might well be imitated by Americans.

The gentleness of the brown folk must also be acknowledged. They speak softly. Even in an argument they do not raise their voices. A low voice is considered the mark of a gentleman. The greater the respect, the lower the voice. Anyone addressed in loud tones considers himself insulted.

Kindness is a paramount virtue. "Is he kind?" may be the first thing a Micronesian will want to know about a stranger.

Missionaries, and Westerners in general, acknowledge somewhat grudgingly that they can actually learn something from the "native." That word, by the way, fell into disrepute for a time. It is now taking on new dignity. It is returning to its proper meaning: a native of a certain place is simply one who was born in that place. I refuse to apologize for use of the word in this book. The cumbersome polysyllabics "indigene" and "indigenous" may properly belong in anthropological papers and annual reports. But in nontechnical writing they are needless affectations. I have never known a native who objected to being called a native. After all, who is not a native? Do we not speak of a native of Hoboken, a native of Canada, a native New Yorker? What is wrong with the expression, "a native-born American"? In Australia a "native" is a white person born in the country as distinguished from one born abroad.

Native is a good, simple, honest word and let's have done with trying to circumvent it by such monstrosities as "indigenous," "aboriginal," and "autochthonous."

It isn't just a matter of semantics. Avoidance of the word "native" is an insult to the native. It implies that there is something wrong with being a native; that he should be ashamed of his native land and of himself.

Is this the way to build up the self-confidence he sorely needs to make the most of the possibilities of his island world?

Happily there is now a tendency not to avoid the word "native" but to give it the pride and nobility that it deserves.

One reason for the increasing tolerance of native ways is that the missionary is more humble than he used to be. Time was when it was a common thing in the Pacific for a missionary to rule the entire life of an island, and rule with a rod of iron.

Now the conduct of island affairs is partly in the hands of the people, partly in those of the alien administration.

In a small outboard the Distad took us to see a missionary at work on the island of Roguron at the far end of the Majuro lagoon. With us was Captain John M. Cotter, skipper of the *Alaska Bear,* 10,000-ton copra freighter docked at Majuro for a full week taking on 3,200 tons of copra.

Cotter endured the bouncing of the small craft with some impatience. He was used to the smooth swing of a heavy ship.

On the surrounding reef which stood only a few feet above sea level, palm trees fought with the wind, native houses swayed on their stilts, and brown children ran back and forth between the thundering ocean shore and the still shore of the lagoon.

The green islands that punctuated the reef were beautiful and fruitful. But the most valuable part of the atoll was the lagoon itself. It was a natural nest for war craft. During the war, battleships, cruisers, destroyers, submarines, and cargo vessels slipped through the narrow breaks in the reef into the safe harbor that coral polyps had built. Seaplanes settled down upon the smooth surface.

At first the vessels were Japanese. Admiral Suetsugu referred to the Micronesian lagoons as "natural aircraft carriers."

Imagine hundreds of such nests covering a sea as wide as the United States and you get some idea of the advantage which Neptune had conferred upon Nippon. The American Pacific between the coast and Hawaii is a vacant waste. The Japanese Pacific was a swarm of naval bases.

It is still a swarm of potential bases, no longer Japanese. Majuro lagoon affords a naval parking lot of a hundred square miles. There are others far larger.

Grinding on the sand a dozen feet short of the beach of Roguron, we waded ashore and walked a mile to the intermediate school. It was a mission school to which boys and girls ranging from eleven to eighteen years of age came from all the islands of the Marshalls.

Here we met Anna Dederer, once the unofficial queen of the island, but now not even the principal of the school. Like most of the remaining missionaries of the American Board in the Trust Territory, her position is now purely advisory. She introduced us to the principal, a Marshallese.

But she is far from idle. She teaches organ, sewing, cooking, theology, and she is also professionally qualified as a nurse and midwife.

We hear the students sing with pipe-organ richness, then go to Anna's house where she, being of German extraction, serves delicious *Obstkuchen* made with the *Obst* most readily available, the banana.

Through a drenching rain we walked back to the shore, peeled off footgear, and waded to the boat. This all struck the ship's captain as absurdly primitive.

The contrast between a little motorboat and a comfortable master's cabin of a 10,000-ton ship was further emphasized in the twenty-mile ride down the lagoon to Majuro. The wind came from dead ahead. The captain and I sat in the bow. The bow was tossed high by every wave, then came down with a pile-driving thump into the trough. It was amazing that water could be so hard. A sudden drop on a cement pavement could not give the body any more of a jolt. In the bow we received not only the full benefit of the pounding, but also heavy showers of spray that soaked me so thoroughly I could wring the water out of my undershirt. Mary, sitting aft, got the spray over the side and though she wore a raincoat with a hood the garment did not close adequately, leaving her with a panel of sea-soaked front from chin to toe. Cotter and I were without raincoats, and I heard the captain swear under his breath:

"Never again in a small boat!"

My bones seemed to drive straight down through the hardwood seat at every hammer blow. Cold rain fell from the skies, salt rain rose from the sea, as we banged along for three endless hours.

"You'll have something to write about anyhow," shivered the captain.

"No," I said, "nobody would believe it."

And that's true. What's so special about riding a boat in rough weather? Nothing to write home about. Such things have to be felt to be appreciated.

(My bottom bone points were as sore as boils the next day.)

We saw another famous missionary and another famous captain, both in the same person—spirited, smiling, seventy-year-old Eleanor Wilson, skipper of the *Morning Star VII* which was moored alongside the *Alaska Bear*.

This was the last of the line of distinguished sailing ships that have carried the Congregational brand of Christianity to the thousand and more islands of the Marshalls.

The ship was about to be sold and Captain Wilson was to be retired to the United States "unless I can persuade them to let me stay on to finish the translation of the Bible into Marshallese."

She failed to persuade them and, shortly after, flew home. So one of the most dramatic chapters in the American conquest of the South Seas was coming to an end. It has been the policy of the ABCFM (American Board of Commissioners for Foreign Missions) to turn over church leadership to native pastors as rapidly as they can be trained.

Catholic policy is quite different. Instead of withdrawing missionaries, the Catholic church sends more year by year. The underlying theory seems to be that the Micronesian pastor, no matter how devoted and competent, lacks the drive and initiative of the white priest.

According to the Assistant Distad, the Christians of the Marshalls are popularly classified as follows. About 20 percent of the Marshallese are considered "true Protestants"; if you attend Christian Endeavor Sunday evening you are a "true Protestant." Ten percent are Catholics. All the rest are known as "far-and-away Protestants." On the day the census taker comes around they report themselves as Protestants, but do not worry about it the rest of the year.

Catholic missions increase in number and authority. Many of the Fathers are dynamos of energy. Father Leonard J. Hacker took us through the modern, well-constructed buildings of the Majuro mission. The mission school was a hive of activity. He took special pride in the blasting power of the lusty student band. He personally conducted the band. The instruments were trombones, trumpets, French horns, tubas, snare drums, bass drums, cymbals, and castanets.

"Where did you get them?"

"From Navy and Army surplus."

"Are you a musician?"

"Not at all."

"Then how did you teach the boys to play?"

"I learned along with them."

To the unaccustomed ear, the chief product of the band seemed to be noise. Nevertheless, playing these difficult instruments as well as they do must give the boys a healthy sense of achievement.

Government schools suffer by comparison with mission schools. It has been Trust policy, made necessary by lack of funds, to let local communities build their own schools. Without either means or experience, the Marshallese have not made a notable success of school construction.

Many of the teachers have not gone through elementary school; practically none have entered the door of a high school.

The UN advises that all teaching should be in English, since in this island world of scores of languages and dialects, a common language is sorely needed. But the harassed Hicom reports that "due to the limited number of Marshallese teachers (less than one percent) who can speak and effectively use English as the language of instruction, Marshallese is still dominant."

Mission schools have done better because they have consistently received funds from America. Now the government schools may begin to catch up following an appropriation of $4,-000,000 by Congress for a school construction program.

This however will not take care of the training of teachers— and a good building with a poor teacher is not a school. In the largest schools an American will teach alongside the Marshallese. The vast majority of schools will have no such help. The road of future education in the Marshalls is long and discouraging.

After twenty years of American presence, few even of the leading citizens can speak or understand English.

I attended a meeting of the Board of Directors of the native-owned firm of Mieco, short for Marshalls Import-Export Company. An American auditor hired by the company made a financial report in English.

The Board members leaned forward with every appearance of rapt attention. They seemed to be drinking in every word. This was most encouraging.

But it was only Marshallese politeness, not understanding. When the auditor had finished, the president, Amata Kabua, repeated the entire report in Marshallese. He alone knew English. From the ten other members, we heard not one word of English all evening.

These men, controlling the largest native firm of the Marshall Islands, were the cream of the educational crop. They were the best product of the headquarters island of the entire Marshall archipelago. In all this great region there were but two university graduates. Amata Kabua was one and the other was Dwight Heine. Needless to say, they did not get their college education in the Marshalls.

Ignorance and superstition still lie like a heavy blanket over the island people. Superstition makes every step of progress more difficult. Dr. John Iaman, a Micronesian, but trained in the British Gilberts, not in the Marshalls, took us about the hospital. He complained:

"Hospital care is free—yet many people who need treatment refuse to come."

"Why is that?"

"They believe that the spirits of those who have died in the hospital are still here."

"Why should that worry them?"

"Because a person is supposed to get mean after he dies. His spirit tries to hurt the living."

"Are there still sorcerers or witch doctors in the Marshalls?"

"There are some fifty or sixty still practicing right here in Majuro atoll. Sometimes they do good. Often if we have a patient with some psychological ailment we advise him to go to a medicine man. The older people have faith in the medicine man's powers, and faith can cure.

"But when it comes to *organic* diseases, these practitioners can do a lot of harm, not only by administering toxic herbs, but by delaying proper treatment. The patient wastes time with them when he is urgently in need of modern care and modern drugs.

"A Marshallese woman who called herself an eye specialist moved about from island to island treating eyes and charging five dollars a patient. Her trick was to remove a piece of metal or glass or other foreign matter from the eye, after first putting it in. Many bad infections resulted, and several cataracts.

"I sent for her and offered her a chance to prove her skill and if she succeeded I would supply her with instruments. She set to work on an eye patient, picking at the eye, and through a magnifying glass we could see that there was no foreign matter there and she was merely plucking at the tissue. She furtively tore off a corner of her fingernail, put it in the eye, then triumphantly picked it out and exhibited it.

"We matched the piece to her fingernail and it fitted exactly. Still she wouldn't admit the trick. We suggested taking her to court and having her perform on a patient there. She balked at that. But apparently the test we had given her frightened her and disillusioned many people, so she has now stopped her malpractice."

In a Majuro home, we found a man lying on the floor mats suffering with a high fever. A Micronesian "health aide," trained in administering simple remedies and instructed to bring serious cases to the hospital, was arguing with the sick man's wife.

"I think you should have your husband go to the hospital."

"But can't you give him something to make him cool?"

"He needs more than that. He should have a doctor."

"Can't the doctor come here?"

"Your husband needs special treatment and care that he can get only in the hospital. Why are you afraid to have him go there?"

"The people who have died there. The hospital is full of their spirits. They never go away and they can be very bad. I am afraid."

It is to the credit of a persuasive health aide and a competent doctor that the man went to the hospital, was cured, and an old superstition lost some of its power.

Superstition sometimes helps. It helped certain missionaries who asked the native captain of a copra ship for permission to come aboard and sing to the crew. He refused.

He soon had reason to regret his refusal. The weather turned bad. You must have good weather to load copra. The missionaries had no sooner left the dock than it began to rain. It poured steadily for two days. To the captain, the reason was plain. Those psalm singers had put a jinx on his ship. He sent his mate to call the missionaries.

"Tell them they can come aboard whenever they please and sing until they bust."

It is only natural that many superstitions have to do with the great, the mysterious, the unpredictable sea.

The American teacher Mrs. Cicely Pickerill, known for half a century as Cy, was traveling through the Mortlock Islands in a small plastic boat. A Mortlock boy was with her.

A rainbow appeared in the sky. It ran north and south.

"That's bad," the boy said. "We're going north, same direction as the rainbow. It could bring us bad luck."

"Don't tell me you believe that old superstition," said Cy. "You know better than that. You've been to school."

The boy was a graduate of George Washington High School on Guam and was at this time on vacation from the University of Hawaii.

But back of him were centuries of tradition that he could not easily shuffle off.

"We won't take chances," he said. "It will do no harm to make a little incantation."

He raised his hand toward the rainbow and repeated a few mystic words. The rainbow vanished.

"You see?" he said. "It works."

On an outing in the country, Cy noticed some of her boys making whistles of reeds. Admiring their initiative, she suggested that they bring their whistles to music class the next day.

The next morning householders within range of the school heard a tremendous chorus of whistling issuing from the music class. They descended upon the school and their spokesman protested:

"This will not do. We want to go fishing today. But this whistling—it will blow up a storm."

Cy, despite her exhaustive knowledge of island ways, had not heard this one before. She apologized for her ignorance. The parents went off, gloomily shaking their heads, casting furtive glances at the sky. Cy prayed for continued good weather. Only so would the people be convinced of the folly of their fears.

But that night Typhoon Lola swept in over the island, tearing fishing boats from their moorings, smashing them against the rocks, ripping thatch roofs from the houses and flattening the pandanus walls, piling the water into waves that rolled over the island and sent the people scurrying up the trees.

The Micronesians are a gentle and forgiving people. They did not blame their beloved teacher. They only said to her sadly:

"Now you know."

6.

The Unfortunate Isles

THE plane circled down to the unhappy lagoon of Jaluit. It had once been the proudest of the atolls. The Japanese made it the capital of the Marshalls.

Since it was nothing but a pile of debris when American bombs had done with it, it was abandoned in favor of Majuro. The Trust sent relief to the homeless inhabitants, evacuated some of them, helped the rest to build shacks and replant crops. The help was well meant but, naturally, inadequate, Jaluit being only one of two thousand islands requiring aid.

Now we go ashore to be immediately surrounded by a circle of scarecrows. The disaster of two decades ago had been abetted by another, this one also coming from the sky.

Typhoon Ophelia had laid almost every palm flat on its back, buried taro plots under coral sand, carried houses aloft like kites, and left nothing but an old Japanese blockhouse built of stone.

Now Jaluit was living on promises, or dying while waiting for them to be fulfilled. The energetic Assistant Distad of the Marshalls had shipped in 36,000 seed nuts, and these had been planted. It was estimated that ten thousand of them would grow and each would bear perhaps sixty nuts a year. But eight years must pass before the first yield

What in the meantime?

§

"King" Juda and his people were evacuated from Bikini because of impending atomic tests in 1946.

Bikini is a coral ring of some twenty islands. The lagoon measures twenty-two miles from east to west, thirteen north to south. The land is comparatively dry but, before the tests, had always provided a fair living. At any rate, it was home and the Bikinians were loath to leave it.

They were moved to Rongerik, an island 130 miles to the east. This action was taken by the Navy without preliminary study of the possibilities of life on Rongerik.

A year passed. There were reports of dissatisfaction but these were regarded as only natural. The authorities were satisfied that the people would settle down and keep quiet.

But at the end of a year "King" Juda had to report that his people were "destitute and unable to support themselves on the island's agriculture or fisheries."

The kindly but busy authorities, again without too much forethought, picked up the dissident monarch and his unhappy people, who hoped that they were to be returned to their home island. Instead they were carried four hundred miles west to Ujelang. In refusing their request to be returned to Bikini, it was explained that the island was still radioactive. Not only were the coconuts contaminated but marine life as well. Fish that fed on algae and other plants in the lagoon became radioactive and many so affected died within three weeks; their decayed bodies passed the contamination back to the plants and this vicious circle might be expected to be continued for many years.

The wrecks of twenty-five warships used as targets in the ma-
neuvers were covered with a radioactive film that could not be
removed and that infected the entire lagoon.

Every island makes different demands upon the ingenuity of
its inhabitants. People who have learned during many generations how to get the best out of one island must learn over
again when transferred to another. They must discover by painful experiment what will grow and what will not, and that may
take years. A Louisiana farmer transplanted to Wyoming could
be no more bewildered than the Bikinians on Ujelang.

Again they were moved, this time six hundred miles southeast to Kili. Kili is not even an atoll, but only a lone island
fully exposed to the fury of the sea.

The refugees appealed to the United Nations. A UN Mission
investigated Kili in 1956, and reported:

> Bikini, with an extensive lagoon, had afforded its people
> the opportunity of making use of an abundance of fish and
> good anchorage facilities for boats, which Kili does not pos-
> sess. Bikini has a larger land area than Kili, which for its
> part has a heavier rainfall and richer soil. On Kili, the
> Bikini people have had to learn new methods of cultivating
> food plants which did not exist in their former habitat.
>
> The lack of a protected anchorage, the unfavorable axis of
> the island with relation to the prevailing trade winds, and the
> narrow shelving reef cause the island to be isolated during
> many months of the year.
>
> Landing conditions are possible only during brief periods,
> between November and late March. The unfavorable surf con-
> ditions consequently prevent the use of sea resources, which
> at best are infinitely poorer than on Bikini, and make the
> loading of copra and landing of merchandise for local con-
> sumption impossible during a large part of the year.

One of the ships that ventured to put in with supplies for the
starving refugees was completely wrecked on Kili's savage reefs.

Another, attempting to take its place, had to limp away to the nearest shipyard for extensive repairs.

Good-hearted but not too practical deskmen came up with another answer—why not let the people of Kili commute to Jabwar to make use of the better fishing and farming facilities available on that island? They were to live at home, but farm and fish in an island three hundred miles away. The Marshallese are famous canoeists, but this was expecting a little too much of them.

They preferred to stay at home and make "Kili bags," an ingenious handwoven article that had caught the fancy of Americans. A paternalistic government encouraged the effort. In fact it brought about a meeting between the bag makers and Walt Disney who offered to buy twenty-five thousand of the bags for sale at Disneyland.

Dismayed by the thought of how much work would be required to make twenty-five thousand bags, the Kilians refused. And since the bags seemed likely to get them in trouble, they stopped making them. This disgusted both the government and Disney. But it seemed logical to the natives. They could not face the prospect of giving up their traditionally independent life for the semi-slavery of regular hours in a great bag factory. They weren't *that* hungry.

It is probable that little more will be done for them. What can you do for people who are too lazy to help themselves? It is soothing to the official conscience to be able to put the blame for the whole unhappy story on the obstinate and uncooperative Bikinian refugees.

℘

Only a little less disgraceful is the Rongelap chapter. The hydrogen bomb test of 1954 surprised the testers. They had specifically assured the Micronesians that the experiments would not affect them in any way. But due to the caprices of wind and weather the population of Rongelap was seriously irradiated by the fallout.

The people were moved to Ejit Island in the Majuro Atoll. There they remained in exile for three years.

The effects of radiation in the case of the Rongelap victims was described by investigators from the UN:

> Penetrating gamma radiation from the ground, trees, and houses, resulted in whole body irradiation. A skin contamination from fallout resulted in spotty localized irradiation of the skin and scalp; and internal contamination occurred from the ingesting of contaminated food and breathing in fallout material.

What the long-term effects might be could not be foretold, but previous experience offers no encouragement. Scientists found that the life span of Hiroshima victims had been seriously shortened by irradiation and there are inconclusive signs of the genetic effect upon future generations.

After three years the Rongelapese were returned to their islands where a new village had been built for them by the Atomic Energy Commission.

ॐ

"All possible precautions" were promised by the AEC, but the skepticism of Micronesians was intensified when an explosion caused a whole island to disappear, leaving a hole a mile wide and nearly two hundred feet deep. Another test so severely exposed twenty-three Japanese fishermen to fallout some eighty miles from the explosion that all were affected and one died. Japan was incensed, not only by this incident but by the fact that copra shipments from the Marshalls carried irradiation to consumers in Japan. Japan had been one of the chief copra markets of the Trust. Now she refused to take any more deliveries without U.S. Navy certification that the copra was not radioactive.

◌

But the tests must go on. The atoll of Eniwetok, once a dream of primitive beauty, has now given way to a military camp where coconut palms have been replaced by talking masts, radar screens, airstrips, warehouses, and laboratories.

Eniwetok consists of thirty islands along the rim of a large lagoon twenty miles by seventeen. It was taken from the Japanese in February, 1944, and used as an air and naval base from which attacks on Japanese bases were launched. It is now a part of the Trust Territory but is the particular charge of the Atomic Energy Commission which has used the island for nuclear tests.

Of course the brown folk who, with their fathers and fathers' fathers as far back as legend can go, had made their home in this atoll, were evicted. They were settled on Ujelang, the island which the Bikinian refugees found unsuitable and intolerable. The protests of the Eniwetok transplants were stilled by a gift of $175,000, and the Trust undertook intensive agricultural projects to make the island fit for human habitation.

◌

The largest atoll in the world, and the chief pride of the people of the 1,150 Marshall islands, was Kwajalein.

The lagoon is sixty-six miles long by eighteen, is deep enough for the greatest ships, affords excellent anchorage, and is protected by a ring of ninety islands.

It is perhaps the most important air and naval base in the entire Trust Territory. Though nominally a part of the Trust, it is really governed by a sort of condominium including the Army, Navy, and the Atomic Energy Commission. It is a maze of machine shops, control towers, radio towers, cranes, docks, and missile trackers—for it is here that the antimissile missiles are being developed.

It swarms like a hill of ants—but white ants, not brown. American airmen, sailors, and scientists push in and out of the supermarkets and line the sixty-foot bar of the Officers' Club.

The Marshallese have been exiled with the exception of those needed for rough work. They live apart in a rusty community known as Tintown. Lest they spread secrets, they are not allowed to leave Kwajalein and other Micronesians may not enter.

&⊌

"Why doesn't the United States test the bombs on its own territory?"

The question has been asked repeatedly by the Marshallese. Through their native Congress they have time and again petitioned the UN for a cessation of nuclear tests in their islands. Critics of the United States take up the matter every year in the UN Trusteeship Council. But the United States harks back to the terms of her contract with the UN: the Trusteeship was to be "strategic," empowering the trustee to use the islands for military purposes.

Quite evidently America is not too happy about all this. Americans are not Frankenstein monsters. They are not sadists delighting in the torture of innocent peoples. They are merely doing what they believe has to be done. They have the law on their side.

But how about the moral law? Surely the Micronesians have some rights in their own islands. In fact these rights are theoretically recognized in the Trusteeship agreement by which the trustee is bound to train the Micronesians to take over their own government at the earliest possible date. The Trust is making an honest effort to bring this about. Yet it collides head on with the military which keeps repeating the word "strategic." What compromise is possible between these two forces?

Intelligent Micronesians understand the American dilemma, yet they resent the use of UN territory for American purposes. America does not own the islands—she is only the trustee temporarily in charge. Micronesians insist that the United States is criminally responsible for displacement of populations and for injury and death caused by radioactive fallout.

America is not wholly to blame. Britain is an accomplice, so long as she relies upon America for nuclear weapons. The Soviet threat spurs the nuclear race. France intensifies the struggle by nuclear experiments in the Sahara and now in the Pacific islands near Tahiti where she is certain to encounter the same flood of native criticism that America enjoys in the Marshalls. Mainland China is edging into the atomic contest. A partial test-ban treaty has had little effect.

This is a nuclear age. Those who want nuclear weapons and those who have them are equally guilty. How the tobogganing toward nuclear disaster is to be halted is a question that no one nation can answer. But the smaller problem of how to carry on experiments without making guinea pigs of helpless and unoffending native peoples is one America must solve if she is to catch up with the march of freedom that has swept Africa and Asia and is now stirring men's minds even in the isolated islands of the Pacific.

7·

Boston in the South Seas

IT is a short trip from Kwajalein to Kusaie, but it transports you to another world.

From pancake-flat Kwajalein where the main crops are rockets and missiles you come to a garden on edge two thousand feet high clothed with nature's own crops of breadfruit, mango, papaya, taro, orange, guava, banana, and a hundred other wild delicacies.

This island was not built inch by inch by coral polyps. It was tossed up out of the sea by volcanic eruptions. And yet it is something of an atoll, being partly encompassed by a lagoon and coral reef. It has both the charm of an atoll and the soaring beauty of tropical mountains.

We enter a small harbor as lovely as an Italian lake. Its still surface reflects romantic peaks that stretch up out of a dark dawn and terminate in sharp stabs of rock blazing in a scarlet sunrise. The fire gradually creeps down the slope, igniting the tops of magnificent palms like matches, one after another.

These mountains stand hand in hand in a semicircle around the little port. They are on the main island of Kusaie. The other semicircle is made up of the small island of Lele, for without its cooperation there would be no harbor. Lele is but an hour's walk around, low, luxuriant, with many sand beaches. In its still morning beauty it looks like a model in wax for exhibition purposes rather than a real island. Hospitable-looking thatch homes nestle in its groves. Canoes line its shore. Yonder on a little point stands a white church, as primly as if cut out of cardboard.

Kusaie might well be a mecca for tourists. Yet it seldom sees a strange face. Planes and ships pass it by. The Trust's reports seldom mention it. Not one in a hundred Trust officials has ever seen it. It is neglected—not willfully—but, after all, it is only one of two thousand islands.

It once had too many visitors. Whalers from Boston and New Bedford circled South America to get into the Pacific, "hanging up their consciences off Cape Horn." They picked up more men along the Pacific Coast. Life aboard a whaler was too hard to attract men, and therefore they were shanghaied. Having been knocked on the head ashore, they woke to find themselves in the forecastle of a ship, seabound. Many of the men recruited in this fashion were a rough lot; and if they were not, the life made them rough. The ships were provisioned for three years and put in at no mainland ports lest the men might escape. Summers, the whale hunters operated in northern waters. Winters, they sailed to the South Seas to rest and riot. When they stepped ashore after months of confinement on a small whaling vessel, they were wild men. Anyone who has spent six months on board ship can perhaps hardly blame them.

Kusaie was discovered by Americans in 1806 and named Strong Island after the governor of Massachusetts. Thus whaling captains of New England learned of the island and thereafter made its beautiful harbor a rendezvous. There were as many as twenty-two whaling ships in this harbor at one time.

The whalers indulged in wild orgies on shore, abducted Kusaie women, and left a legacy of foreign diseases. The population dwindled from about two thousand when first discovered to two hundred in late Spanish times.

Here, according to an account written in 1899 by the ethnographer F. W. Christian, "the famous 'Bully' Hayes, the modern buccaneer, played fine pranks after losing his beautiful vessel on the reefs, half frightening the lives out of the peaceful Kusaians by landing a number of fierce and warlike Ocean and Gilbert Islanders, who brewed huge quantities of coconut-toddy, and set the whole place in a ferment with their carousals and mad orgies. Night after night they kept it up, alternately drinking and fighting. Murdered men's bodies were picked up on the beach every morning, and the poor natives of Lele fled in terror of their lives."

When the American buccaneers of the whaling fleet had done their worst and only a pitiful remnant was left of the Kusaie people, there came other Americans, also buccaneers in a fashion, and also from Boston, to repair the damage done by their countrymen.

It was a romantic and pioneering venture. American Sunday-school children contributed their dimes to make possible the great square-rigged sailing ship *Morning Star*, which should carry their missionaries to the South Seas to convert the heathen. Of course there were plenty of heathen in Boston. But they did not wear grass skirts and lop off heads. Surely it was the buccaneer spirit in so far as it means the fascination of far seas, the courage to sail them, and the boldness to take captives, that prompted both the children and the missionaries. The project gripped the imagination. The Micronesian mission thereafter never lacked for funds. As soon as one *Morning Star* was wrecked, another was fitted out. There were seven in all.

For eighty-four years, missionaries of the American Board of

Boston have been at work in Kusaie. Let us go ashore and see
the results.

We walk down the village street, through a sea of seraphic
smiles. There are low bows and soft good mornings. All the
inhabitants are in long white robes as in the realms of the blest.
Houses are so neat that they ache. Music drifts about—
whistled, hummed, twanged—hymn tunes familiar in New
England churches.

A group of young men approached us. One of them, a fine,
erect figure of particularly noble appearance, came toward us
with a broad smile and an open hand.

"I am Paul," he said. It was not necessary for him to say more.
We knew that the young man so modestly introducing himself as
"Paul" was the king of Kusaie.

The South Sea king is still a king, but his rule is not as of
old. Behind him and a little above him is the District Administrator. So long as the brown king does not question this higher
authority, he is permitted to rule his people. This is not out of
any kindness to him, but because the overlords have discovered
that the easiest way to govern the natives is through their own
tribal rulers.

The fact that the island king is able to adjust himself with
dignity to this situation of ruling, and being ruled, is a tribute
to his kingliness.

His blood is truly royal. For centuries his family has provided the people with kings. The result is an inherited poise
and manner, a regal gentlemanliness, in contrast to the brisk,
brusque ways of some foreign petty officials of common family
who have been trained but not bred.

This system of governing by proxy is not new. The Spaniards
used it, the Germans used it, the curt Japanese irritated the
people less and got more cooperation by filtering their orders

through the native ruler whom the people respected and loved.

The native kings, with few exceptions, have been modest men. I remembered Paul's father, King John. When I had met him he had handed me his calling card. On it was printed, K. J. SIGRAH. Sigrah was his family name.

"What does the K. J. stand for?" I asked.

"King John," he admitted. "But you may call me just K. J."

Though humble, few kings are ever servile. More than once the kings have risked their own safety in championship for their people. The Kusaians remember when King John was held all day in the Japanese government office while a battery of officials tried to wring from him a promise to enforce a law he thought to be unreasonable. Finally, when the schoolteacher went out on the veranda and saw that several hundred angry Kusaians had gathered around the office to learn what had become of their king, he was released.

Every other inch a king in authority, he is every inch a king in loyalty to his people. The kings of the South Seas have been an indispensable link between the new and the old. They are generally sufficiently intelligent to appreciate the advantages of the foreigner's more scientific way of doing things—and yet they understand perfectly the traditional psychology and customs of the people.

"We knew your father," I said, "but not you."

King Paul smiled. "If I was alive then I was too small to be noticed."

"Your father and his ancestors did wonders for Kusaie."

"I know. But they had the help of the missionaries."

Together, the kings and the missionaries had performed a miracle. Once an island dreaded for its savagery and brutality, where shipwrecked strangers were sure of prompt death, where a king and his henchmen were carried in their canoe to a great hole and buried alive, where American whalers murdered and were murdered, where American ships were sunk in the harbor, where disease and violent death reduced the population from two thousand to two hundred, Kusaie became an unbelievable isle of twelve hundred angels.

"I remember your father told me that in the old times there used to be one or two hundred murders a year. But during his lifetime there had not been a single native murder. I asked him how many people were in jail. He said there was no jail. I asked him what was done with disorderly fellows who drank a little too much. He said there was no drinking on Kusaie. And practically no smoking. No divorces. No house of ill fame. I had never known such a place. It seemed quite incredible."

"I'm afraid we have slipped since then," said King Paul. "You hear that?" The jukebox of a nearby bar was pouring out a sexy ditty straight from Tin Pan Alley. "There was never anything like that when I was a boy. But things have changed. In some ways it's better."

I agreed, and told him about the Misses Baldwin and the 250 phonograph records. The story was new to Paul, who had been too young at the time to take an interest in such things.

Miss Baldwin and Miss Baldwin were large, strong-faced women whose fortitude belied their ages of seventy-six and seventy-eight. They were in charge of a mission school on the far shore of Kusaie where eighty-eight young men and women ranging from thirteen to twenty years in age were being taught reading, writing, and religion. We paddled the eight miles to see them.

The school was a dingy barn of a place perched on a hilltop with a magnificent view of lagoon and sea. It had the feeling of being completely removed from the world and all its wiles. Magazines did come from America but all pictures of women in low-necked or close-fitting gowns were clipped out before the journals were allowed to reach the eyes of Kanaka youths. The cult of the throttle-necked and ankle-length mother hubbard prevailed. The missionaries had not been off the island in twenty-five years. In 1911 they went to America and got a dress pattern; the dresses of the girls had been cut from it ever since.

My wife made a break.

"How much material does it take for one of the girls' dresses?" she asked.

"Six yards," replied the elder Miss Baldwin.

"Oh, that must be expensive. One of my dresses takes only three yards."

Miss Baldwin stiffened. "It is never expensive to cover the body," she said.

Two hundred and fifty phonograph records of the lighter sort were sent by well-meaning friends in America. The missionaries took them to an upper room, locked the door, removed the horn from the phonograph so that no sound might escape from the room, and played the records through. Then they dispatched them by boat to a point far outside the reef whose bottom is said to be a good mile down, quite beyond the reach of the best native diver, and consigned them to the deeps.

Although reared in the liberal Congregational tradition, the ladies were won over by the mysterious island silences to the conviction that the second coming of the Lord was close at hand. In a world of increasing wickedness, they saw all the prophecies being fulfilled.

"Apart from the world on this little island, we feel that perhaps we can see such things more clearly than those who are in the midst of the false teachings."

Both of these devoted women gave their lives for Kusaie, and the elder gave her eyes as well. She translated the entire Bible into the Kusaian language. She broke her glasses and sent the prescription to England to be refilled. In the meantime the proofs were ready to read. She felt that the natives must not be made to wait for their Bible. So she read the proofs . . . and went blind.

The book was manufactured at the school. The girls set the type, the boys printed it. The hand-sewing alone took two years. Only three copies could be bound in a day. But the great work was completed and the Kusaians had their Bible. The blind translator placed her hand upon the great three-inch-thick volume, her monument, and in her peaceful, unseeing face there was no regret.

She went on translating—arithmetics, grammars, Bible helps. Her sister read aloud the English version and she dictated the Kusaian. Of course in addition to these cloistered tasks there was the schoolwork to supervise—the daily guidance of eighty-eight inquiring minds. The curriculum might be lopsided, the pedagogy faulty, but the devotion was superb. A flaming object lesson for the Japanese official, or for any other official, for that matter, who is supposed to exist for the good of the people.

Robert Louis Stevenson expressed it well when he said:

> Those who have a taste for hearing missions, Catholic or Protestant, decried, must seek their pleasure elsewhere than in my pages. Whether Catholic or Protestant, with all their gross blots, with all their deficiency of candor, of humor, and of common sense, the missionaries are the best and most useful whites in the Pacific.

And now the majority of the "most useful whites" are gone. The missionaries have been replaced by native pastors. This is in harmony not only with the policy of the Protestant churches but that of the Administration—to train the islanders for self-government.

It doesn't work perfectly. The people don't understand democracy. Why should they? For centuries they were under the rule of kings. The missionaries also were autocrats. The first missionary, the Reverend B. G. Snow, even tried to boss the king. When King George rose in church to express his own opinions, he was told sharply to sit down. There were many trials of strength between the two dictators. At the first benediction Snow asked the people to stand. They did not stir. Their eyes turned to their king. Tradition required that they should never stand without their king's permission. King George enjoyed the missionary's discomfiture. He allowed a long, painful pause before he languidly rose to his feet and commanded the people to stand. They stood.

King George bought Western articles from the whalers and paid for them with women. He tried to keep this trade a secret from Snow. But Snow had his spyglass trained on the harbor and when he saw women go aboard the vessels he immediately followed and berated the sinful whalers.

The women went ashore and the whalers followed them. The angry missionary armed with a whip spent half of every night driving them out of the native houses.

Yet in some ways the whalers played into the missionary's hands. The missionary required that all attendants in church be clothed. But the people complained that they had no clothes and therefore could not attend church. The whalers soon took advantage of this situation. They brought bolts of cotton to Kusaie and traded them for female favors. The net result was that more people came to church.

The Kusaians now have their own island legislature which serves as a school of democracy. This would work better if the presiding officer were a commoner. But who should be elected magistrate but King Paul himself! Thus the shreds of aristocracy are jealously preserved. King Paul makes a visible effort to encourage the legislators to think for themselves and express themselves freely. But when some proposal he has made meets with unexpected opposition, he reverts instinctively to the age-old authority of Kusaian kings. He brings down his fist hard and says:

"I, Paul, demand it."

The legislature promptly bows to the divine right of kings and democracy goes fluttering out the window.

8.

Forgotten Venice

A SORRY victim of neglect is the mysterious city in the sea off the coast of Ponape. One of the world's most remarkable archaeological treasures is being allowed to fall into ruin.

Egypt is proud of its pyramids, Peru protects the palaces of the Incas, little Cambodia spares no expense to guard Angkor Wat. Yet here is something comparable in mystery and majesty that the richest nation on earth "can't afford to preserve." Does America respect nothing but the new?

Far more notable than the stone statues of Easter are the ruins of Nan Madol. But Easter is known, Nan Madol is unknown. Anyone has been free to step ashore on Easter. Nan Madol until now has been part of the secret world—shut away by the Germans until World War I, the Japanese until World War II, the Americans until the present relaxation of "strategic restrictions."

Nan Madol (alternate spelling, Nanmatal) is still largely hidden—not by official cover-up, but by jungle. Here is an amazing prehistoric city of one hundred man-made islands squared into city blocks and intersected by water streets. The city covered eleven square miles. All traffic was by boat along the Venice-like canals.

Abruptly from the water's edge rise beetling castle walls made up of vast natural prisms of basalt larger than the stones used in the Pyramids. The mighty building blocks which compose these barbaric structures make the English castles or those of the Rhine seem delicate and ladylike in comparison. The ferocious appearance is heightened by the fact that there has been no effort to join the stones. I have tried unsuccessfully to insert a knife blade between the perfectly matched stones of Inca structures in Peru. Here one might insert a hand or a head with ease. The difference is that the Inca stones were tooled to fit. But no tool has touched these stones. The material would have defied Inca implements. And the old-time ax of the South Seas made of Tridacna shell was too brittle to chisel this igneous rock.

Then how was the material hewn into these great blocks? It was not hewn. It was used just as nature made it. In many parts of Ponape may still be found basalt fashioned by the volcanic fires of long ago into the form of massive columnar prisms, six-sided, often twenty-five feet or more in length, and from three feet to twelve feet in diameter.

Thus the building blocks were ready made and only needed to be transported. But what a mighty task to transport them! Most of them were brought fifteen miles or more from the neighborhood of the great cliff of Chokach. There is no sign that the wheel was known and there were no beasts of burden. Craft very different from the present canoes must have been necessary. Probably great rafts were used. To raise the stones to their positions must have been a herculean task even with the aid of an inclined plane and unlimited manpower.

Our launch, drawing only a few inches of water, could barely scrape through the choked canals. We had to get out to lift trees so that the boat might slide under. Huge basalt blocks had fallen into the liquid street.

It had been bad enough on our first visit, during the Japanese regime. Now it was worse. We landed at Nan Tauach, the Place of Lofty Walls. We entered a court through a gateway flanked by two cliffs built of monstrous stones that looked as if they had come from the Giant's Causeway.

PONAPE

This awesome place had evidently been the chief temple of the city. The vast court open to the sky had been kept cleared of jungle by the Japanese. But now, what a sorry sight! Seeds had grown into shrubs, shrubs had grown into trees, the trees had become giants. The great walls were being systematically wrecked by the coiling roots. Cyclopean stones had tumbled in heaps. We climbed to the top of the battlements that remained, and looked in vain for the rest of the city. It had been swallowed bodily by jungle.

We descended to the underground vault which, according to the speculations of German archaeologists, was used by the priests to practice their mumbo jumbo. It was half buried under columns of basalt twenty-five feet long and three feet through. Each must weigh as much as a locomotive. Squirming between them, we dropped into the vault. It was cluttered with debris. Blocks uprooted by the trees had fallen into it. Many priceless artifacts had been found here by German and Japanese scientists. Now all the past was covered by the chaotic present.

It had not been visited in a long time, even by natives, who have the belief that any one entering it will surely die. They tell the story of the German governor, Baron Berg, who perished of a mysterious illness immediately after he had invaded this holy of holies.

On foot we tried to penetrate other parts of the city, precariously crossing canals on fallen trees. We could get only occasional glimpses of structures well known to the Germans—the king's palace, the feast house, the city hall, the arsenal, the house of the soothsayers, the forts, the burial place of the kings.

The Smithsonian Institution some years ago cleared small areas with the purpose of constructing a diorama of the city for exhibit in Washington. These areas had been promptly choked by new growth and when some critics scored the Administration for not continuing and expanding the clearance project, the reply was made:

"We have only so much money. Should we spend it on schools and hospitals, or ruins?"

And so it comes back, as always, to that harassed congressman from Maine or Alabama who is naturally more interested in a new fire hall for the state capital than in faraway wonders three thousand years old.

We must depend upon studies made by the inquisitive Germans for our knowledge of Nan Madol.

It seems clear that the city was built up out of the lagoon as a Venice, and is not a land city that has sunk. It was not built by the race now here. People contented with palm thatch for all buildings, private or public, could hardly have conceived, much less erected, these structures. Stone barricades and walls are not unknown among the Micronesians but usually they are made of the sort of stones a farmer takes from his field and piles in a fence. It would be easier to build a whole fort thus than to move just one of these blocks from its place in the mountains to the stone Venice. There is no record of the brown people ever having made use of the mammoth basaltic prisms in their buildings.

The city appears to have been constructed by a black race. This conclusion was reached by Kubary on the basis of measurements of calvaria, or tops of skulls, found beneath the ruins. The measurements were found to be entirely different from those of the modern inhabitants of Ponape and showed negroid characteristics. It is evident that these were people of a superior civilization. The structures are reminiscent of another black marvel, the palace of Saint Christophe, in Haiti.

There is no history of the ruins. They are remotely prehistoric so far as the people of Ponape are concerned—people whose collective memory runs back only a little way, since, having been illiterate, they have no written records. But while there is nothing that can be called history, there are legends that have been passed down from generation to generation.

According to the weavers of legends, the origin of the city in the sea is easily explained. Two demigods, Olochipa and Olochopa, built the city. They caused the mighty columns of basalt to fly through the air from the great rock of Chokach, and by the same magic, they floated them into position to form these mighty structures with walls fifteen feet thick. This building project, which might have taken humans a hundred years to complete, was finished between one breath and the next. The two semi-deities moved in as joint kings, ruling not only the city but all of the great island of Ponape.

Olochipa died and Olochopa ruled alone. When he was on his deathbed he appointed his military chieftain, Sauteleur, king of Ponape.

Twelve generations of Sauteleurs ruled Ponape—and now there begins, perhaps, to be some truth in the legends, for the names of the later kings are known and many details concerning their characters and achievements. They were ruthless dictators. One in particular, Sakon Mwei, was so cruel and oppressive that "a man on the far side of the island dared not harvest so much as a louse from his own head without paying the appropriate tribute to the king in Nan Madol."

For twelve generations there were no wars to fight. The ruling classes in the capital city became rich beyond imagination and lolled in luxury. Their life was easy and soft. Their military arts were forgotten.

Therefore they fell an easy prey to the ancestors of the modern Ponapeans who came up from the south under a warrior chief, Iso-ka-lekel.

At first the invaders were repelled with great losses and retreated toward the sea. This retreat was halted by a brave lieutenant, Nanparatak, who drove a spear through his foot into the ground, determined not to retreat another step. His companions rallied around him and again they approached the formidable ramparts.

As they hesitated, not knowing how to launch their attack, a native woman came to speak with Iso-ka-lekel. She had been cast out of the king's household, and jealousy prompted her to reveal the military weakness of the city and to instruct the invader how he and his men might enter the palace and take the king unaware.

Under cover of night the brown warriors wormed their way into the palace. They found the king at the great altar (which can still be seen). They murdered him and his guards and proceeded with a massacre of the city's inhabitants.

Some of the women they took as wives. That is said to be the reason for a noticeable black strain in Ponape blood today. The old civilization was stamped out. The island metropolis was abandoned. The brown race established itself in the jungles of Ponape, there to remain practically unchanged to this day.

Nan Madol is a city of ghosts. Ponapeans give it a wide berth. They say that spirits walk the towering battlements by night. Some profess not to believe this.

When we asked one chief whether he took this superstition seriously he laughed and replied, "Of course not. I am a Christian."

"Then you would enter Nan Madol without fear—even at night."

"Certainly."

"Would you go with us tonight?"

"I am very sorry. I go to prayer meeting tonight."

"Then tomorrow night?"

"No," he smiled. "It's not that I am afraid. It's just that—well—you understand."

We really had not planned to visit Nan Madol by night. It's not that we shared the old superstitions or stood in fear of ghosts and spirits and such . . . but . . . you understand.

Nan Madol can never be forgotten by one who has visited it. Its mystery grips the imagination, and its archaeological impor-

tance in the prehistory of the Pacific demands that it be preserved and some attempt made to unravel its secrets. The
Trust's annual report published in 1964 frankly states that
"there has been no major restoration or preservation work."

And none is promised.

9.

Fear

I SAT in the office of Richard Umhoefer, Acting Distad of Ponape. An old Ponapean came in. He bowed until his head was on a level with his hips.

"You go right out and come in again," said Umhoefer. "And don't bow. You know that's not Ponapean custom. Why do you do it?"

The old man grinned sheepishly. He went out and came in again. With difficulty he held himself erect. He stated his business and left.

"Why did you object to his bowing?"

"We don't want servility. If these people are ever going to govern themselves they will have to get the idea of equality and self-reliance. Bowing is un-American and un-Ponapean."

"If it's not Ponapean, where did they get it?"

"Japanese officials made them bow. The Germans were even more high and mighty. When a German drove by every Ponapean must remove his hat. Or be flogged."

"But I notice the young people don't bow and scrape."

"No, and that's good. Because they are the ones who will have to take over when we leave."

The magnificent island of Ponape reminds one of Tahiti. Girdled by a lagoon which in turn is circled by a coral reef, Ponape is the second largest island in the entire Trust Territory and rises like a great green pyramid to its central peaks half a mile high. It is well watered because its mountains snare the clouds. Like Tahiti, it is rich in waterfalls leaping from breathtaking cliffs. The mighty rock of Chokach, nine hundred feet high, guards the main harbor.

This huge natural fortress, two-thirds the height of Gibraltar, drops away in basaltic cliffs so steep that they can be scaled only in one place. There the Japanese constructed a dangerous trail. They mounted heavy batteries on the flat crown commanding the lagoon.

More than once in the past this rock has been used as a stronghold. In German times a governor noted for his harsh methods came to Ponape to put down a native rebellion. When he had the king arrested and flogged, the islanders retaliated by assassinating him, his secretary, and all of his higher officials. Then they fled to Chokach and pulled themselves up by lianas to its summit. But German soldiers trained in wall-scaling tactics climbed the precipice and captured the natives. Some were executed, others deported to Palau.

Chokach looms up like a vast organ, its basaltic columns resembling the pipes. It rises higher than the similar basaltic pipe organ of Wyoming known as the Devil's Tower, the first wonder of nature to be made a national monument in the United States. It is reminiscent also of Fingal's Cave in which columns of basalt soar like the pillars of a cathedral. Basalt, lava once molten and cooled to form prisms, is one of the most fine-grained, hardest, and heaviest of all rocks. No wonder the present builders of Ponape have preferred roofs of thatch and walls of woven pandanus.

Basalt is still used however for one purpose. Basalt stones line the inside of an earth oven. Coral rock would be cracked and crumbled by the heat. Basalt was born in a volcano and to it heat means nothing.

৵
৵

Ponape is now ready for visitors with a fine new hotel. On our first visit there was no such facility. This was advanced as a cogent reason why we must remain on board while the ship was in port. We could not have landed if we had not acquired a princely patron.

A young man in amber glasses and golf pants had asked us to join him in a game of deck golf. He spoke English surprisingly well. When I remarked on it he said that he had spent some time in England. It was only later that we learned he had been educated at Oxford. He had a frank friendly manner, quite different from the clamlike inscrutability of many Japanese. He did not play deck golf with consummate skill and Mary soon put him in the "pool." She was called "nasty" for her pains.

When he had gone to his cabin, the steward came to tell us rather breathlessly that he was Prince Saionji, grandson of the last of the Genro, the elder statesmen who guided the policy of the nation until the militarists seized power. At this time his grandfather was the most influential and most respected man in Japan, hardly excepting the Emperor.

The young prince, not yet thirty, occupied himself in the treaties department of the Japanese Gainusho, Foreign Office. He was distinctly pro-American and pro-British and loved to talk with anyone acquainted with Europe or America. He had various fine plans, one of them to establish a university like Oxford in Japan.

We soon found that we had gained a powerful ally. We were of course the only American passengers on this ship, as we had been on all the others, and the closely enveloping Japanese atmosphere had sometimes been very oppressive. Now the lowering brows lifted, the Japanese politeness one reads about began to take the place of the more usual Japanese rudeness, and suddenly nothing was too good for us.

Land on Ponape? Why of course. A radiogram was sent to the governor and he radioed back that a house had been placed at our disposal. It was not much of a house but it commanded an astounding view of the island-studded harbor, towering Chokach, and the gleaming white reef. Fruits of every description drooped from the trees around the cottage. Ponape is one of the best-watered islands in the entire Pacific. Anything will grow here, including mold and madness. Telephone poles sprout branches.

A man was slashing out some jungle undergrowth that was encroaching upon the garden.

"It comes in at the rate of a foot or two every day," said the governor. "And perhaps you haven't believed the stories you've heard about Ponape telephone poles turning into trees. Well, look at that one." Sure enough, the pole before our house was leafing out lustily.

"But I'll tell you something stranger than that," he went on. "The director of our experimental farm stuck his walking stick into the ground. It was made of green wood. That was two years ago. Now it's a tree."

The Spaniards called Ponape "the garden island" and made it their headquarters for all Micronesia. An early visitor described the island as "of a prodigious and inexhaustible fertility." Sago palms, bananas, mangoes, orange and lime trees grow in greatest magnificence. Beds of wild ginger carpet the ground, sending up a pungent aromatic reek from their trodden leaves. There is no lack of food in the land, for yams and taro are zealously cultivated.

The overwhelming lushness and lavishness of growth on Ponape has had a profound effect upon the people. This is more or less true anywhere. Man's life is influenced by the life around him. Many of his habits and superstitions are determined by the trees and shrubs; and this is curiously illustrated in some of the folkways of the Ponape natives.

The jungle is their medicine chest and source of magic. A decoction of the leaves of the *inot* is prized as an aphrodisiac. The *yol*, a giant convolvulus, is said to enable a woman to accomplish abortion. The *chenchul* facilitates childbirth. The astringent *ioio* is a specific for sore throat. Take *ingking* for colic. The seaweed *kom* is a narcotic. The pounded bark of *tupuk* will heal a wound. The bushweed *or* will reduce fever. *Par* is a tonic. *Ngi* will cure dysentery. It is claimed that *maikon* purifies the blood. *Kava* brings narcotic oblivion; and the highly poisonous, quick-acting *kiti* makes suicide almost a pleasure.

Black paint comes from the candlenut tree or *chakan,* varnish from the *ais,* thatch from the coconut or the pandanus, shutters from a lovely reed grass called *alek,* house posts from the giant fern, *katar,* perfume from the polypody fern, *kitau,* boats from the *pulok,* flutes from the reed *ro*—and clothing has been until recently so commonly made from tree bark that one word for clothes is *kun-ne-kai* meaning skin of trees.

Dean of the plant world of Ponape is the giant banyan. It starts life on a shoestring, as a slender vine twining among the branches of a tree and feeding upon it. This parasitic vine drops aerial roots which clasp the trunk of its host and finally strangle it. The original tree dies inside the new one which now has its own roots firmly in the ground. The vine has become a tree. From its rapidly spreading branches it continually drops new aerial roots to sway in the breeze until they finally reach the ground and worm their way into it, each forming a new trunk to support the constantly expanding canopy. The insignificant little sprig that came to dinner and stayed may at last cover an acre, blotting out all other growth.

So extraordinary a tree is naturally regarded with superstitious awe.

Animals too are feared, even worshipped. You must not use the actual name of certain sacred animals. Evasive polite names are substituted.

The centipede is inhabited by a spirit that will be deeply offended and retaliate with a severe nip if you use its common name. You must learn two ceremonial titles. In daylight the centipede must be called *Man-en-ran,* the Creature of the Day. After dark it should be referred to as *Man-en-pong,* the Creature of the Night.

A particularly unpleasant green eel, the *macho,* must be mollified by certain rites. Legend tells the origin of the deadly macho. Long ago a cruel chief murdered his wife and children. His neighbors drove him into a swamp where he escaped by changing into an eel. The spirit of a dead chief becomes a minor god. And since the chief was wicked, the god of the macho is wicked.

This eel is as much at home on land as in the water. It may climb a mangrove tree and wait to pounce upon any prey passing below. While we were in Ponape a man bitten by a macho was brought to the hospital. He died after two days. His friend explained his death—he had not been properly respectful to the god-eel.

Another savage eel is found only in fresh water. Here again, the real name, *it,* is taboo and the animal is addressed by the more respectful name, *Kamichik,* the Terrible One. On the Kiti uplands, three thousand feet above the sea, there is a lake filled with this writhing death. Christian natives of Mortlock identify this eel as the serpent of the Garden of Eden.

The lizard is lord of many quaking hearts, for he is the abode of the devil. The Ponape natives spend much effort trying to please the evil one in the savage red-spotted black lizard known as *kieil*. And it would seem most unfortunate that the god of carpentry should choose to live in a mean tree lizard, so that if a man wishes to build a house or a canoe he must first seek out this animal, no matter how hard to find, and pray for success. Otherwise he fears that the lizard-god will come in the night and destroy what he has done during the day.

There is an alligatorlike skink that haunts burying grounds and feeds upon corpses—which distresses the natives, not because the bodies have been eaten, but because the spirits of the dead men will be angry and will return to avenge themselves upon their relatives.

A prickly green lizard called *man-tau-och,* meaning "animal-go-up-ivory-palm-tree," possesses an uncanny ability, it is said, of making any man who climbs this lofty tree become dizzy and fall. So a native will not go up a tree in which this animal is seen.

Birds also control man. The albatross has mysterious powers. Never go near the *orra,* for this black nocturnal bird is the god of death and disease. The *limokon* is a bird of prophecy. If you hear its cry on your right, you may go on, if on your left, you must turn back or your trip will lead to disaster.

The shark is a god and must be obeyed. The blue starfish, say the Ponape folk, will bring rain if it is plucked out of the lagoon—and that would be a pity since Ponape already gets more rain than it wants. If an expectant mother eats a certain spotted fish, the baby will be spotted.

The coral shelves of the Ponape lagoon are the home of the

Favorite Wife of the Flame Tree, as the sea slug is respectfully called.

Perhaps the most feared aquatic divinity is the stingray. Its real name in Ponape is *pae,* but that must not be spoken. It is referred to reverentially as Queen of the Sea Bottom. The queen, as becomes royalty, does not exert herself unduly. She lies passively on the bottom and waits for her dinner to be served. She is protected by a bared bayonet projecting upward from her tail—and if a wading native steps on this poisonous saw-toothed blade, the outcome may very easily be fatal.

The islanders' superstitious dread of the stingray is so great that until recently a Yap wizard could capitalize on it and use the spine in his eerie business. He made a wand of the vicious spine. By waving it in the air while chanting an incantation, he could either curse or cure. If you wished your neighbor to die, you had but to pay the wizard's fee and he would wave the doomed man to death. If your neighbor did not obligingly die, the wizard would supplement his magic arts with something less magical and more effective—possibly the ministration of a little poison, or the placing of another stingray, point up, in the victim's bed where he might roll upon it in his sleep.

On the other hand, if you were ill, and had the necessary fee, the *machamach,* as the wizard was called, could wave a stingray wand and cure you. If you were not cured you would not dare admit it.

Fear. Fear. Fear. Fear is the constant refrain of savage life. Dread of the gods of sun and moon, of wind and sea, of rock and soil, and particularly of man's closest and best neighbors, the animals and plants. Rousseau depicted the "son of nature" as free and happy. How many "sons of nature" had he personally encountered? The savage does not understand his surroundings. To be ignorant is to be afraid. Animism, which places a malicious spirit in every growing thing, is man's first effort to explain nature. When man learns, animism fades, science takes its place. As his scientific knowledge grows, so grows his realization that nature is his friend.

The change is taking place in Ponape. Young people are cynical about the beliefs of their elders. And yet, when it comes right down to it, they are inclined to do and say the safe thing. Why take chances?

A pavement twenty feet wide, once the main street of a busy Japanese town, now lies neglected and almost completely swallowed by jungle.

No pattern is necessary and no expense is involved in the making of a grass skirt.

In theory education is "compulsory," yet lack of roads
and lack of schools make education impossible for many.

The pig gets the affection that people of other climes lavish upon the dog and cat.

This is American architecture as the Micronesian sees it. Quonsets house the bank, land office and post office in Truk.

The ironclad, warehouselike government administration building on Truk scarcely does credit to the flags of the United States and United Nations.

She is a high school graduate and a trained nurse. She wore a Sears Roebuck dress while in high school, but does not believe in putting on airs (or unnecessary clothing) in her native village. A baby snuggles under the blanket.

Heavy—about fifty pounds. A stone coin of this size was bought by the Money Museum of a Detroit bank for $75.

Weather custom-made. Witch doctor Yonolang will blow
one conch to produce sunshine, if that's what you want—
another to bring rain.

The agricultural director of Truk has successfully grown dwarf coconut trees which make it unnecessary to climb to dangerous heights to harvest the nuts.

A judge doesn't need a black robe to be wise. Judge Leon is one of the most highly respected in the islands.

A traditional South Sea home. The thick thatch keeps out the heat, the porous walls admit air.

The white man's "improvement"—a graceless box with an iron roof, turning the room into a bake oven. The occupants retreat outdoors or *under* the house.

Pakin, a typical atoll. Lagoon on the right, deep sea on left, the girdling coral reef dotted with islands.

10.

Meet Ag

WE had not been on Ponape an hour before we were asked, "Have you seen Ag?"

"No," I said, visualizing some eccentric female character. "Who is she?"

Ag's identity was explained. Americans, notorious time-savers, abbreviate whenever possible. A District Administrator is a "Distad," the High Commissioner is the "Hicom." "Ag" is the Agricultural Experiment Station.

We were taken to meet Ag. In charge was young Leo Migvar, with a B.S. in agriculture from Washington State University and a D.T.A. in tropical agriculture from the Imperial College of Tropical Agriculture in Trinidad.

He took us about the 23-acre farm, the only familiar feature of which was the handsome, castlelike Japanese laboratory building, now an empty shell.

❦

I remembered the place as it had been. Japan had accomplished an agricultural revolution on this very spot. The Japanese, of course, are expert farmers. They are used to getting large yields from little land. They do it by handwork, not by machine. Just such handwork is necessary in the islands. The climate is more or less like that in the Japanese homeland—in fact the heat is more intense in some interior valleys of Japan than in sea-cooled islands near the equator.

A clever farmer named Hoshino was given the job of developing this experimental farm. No one expected much of him. The vegetable was practically unknown in Micronesia and experts had said it could not be raised there because of the heat and moisture. Hoshino imported vegetables from Japan, coddled them, lost some of them, but succeeded in acclimatizing the cucumber, eggplant, tomato, radish, okra, lettuce, carrot, onion, squash, pumpkin, melon, watermelon, ginger-cabbage, kohlrabi, pea, bean, spinach, mitsuba, potato, sweet potato, sugar potato, and eight-headed potato.

And fruits, flowers, exotic trees! One might imagine himself in the Garden of Allah as he wandered through Hoshino's experimental farm. Here were plant immigrants from all lands. It was like a world convention of growing things. Hoshino, bluff, hearty, rubber-booted, accompanied us as we walked about.

He pointed out corn from Kansas, chestnuts from Polynesia, cashew nuts from India, cloves and nutmeg from Celebes, alligator pears from Hawaii, lichee nuts from China, Brazil nuts from Brazil, oranges from California, jackfruit from Malaya, mangosteen and pomegranate from Borneo, aloes from Africa. Java had sent many delegates: the sapodilla plum, coromandel gooseberry, vanilla, pepper, cinnamon. And here were rubber trees, mahogany, teak, sago palm, oil palm, peacock palm, sugar palm.

There was a whole garden of drug trees—caiupute, tamarind, benzoin, and the like. "When I have some small ailment, I don't need to go to the drugstore," said Mr. Hoshino. "I come here and fill my own prescription with some bark or sap or leaves from this pharmacy."

Altogether in this farm there were 238 fruits, vegetables, grasses, shrubs, and trees that had not formerly been native to Ponape—but were now! Nothing was kept that did not become indigenous, that had to be propagated by new supplies of seeds from abroad.

Many of the plants were synthetic, Burbanked, or Hoshino-ized. Rice, for example. Rice needs dry weather when harvested. But there is no such thing as dry weather in Ponape. However, the rice of India is accustomed to a wet harvest period, but it lacks other qualities of the Japanese variety. Mr. Hoshino took us down to flourishing rice fields.

"Here," he pointed to anemic rice that looked up disconsolately into a black sky from which great drops were even then rattling down, "is Japanese rice. This is a patch of Indian rice, not much better. But all the rest of the field is the crossbreed of those two."

The child was half as tall again as either of its parents, and had fine, heavy kernels. It combined the good breeding of the Japanese rice with the rain-defying hardihood of the Indian.

All the wealth of good things developed by the trial farm was available to the native. Some rather brutal persuasion was employed at times to get him to make use of his privileges. Village delegations were brought to the farm, instructed, and supplied with seeds, and an expert went back with them to see that the seeds were used. Every school had a farm, equipped from the trial farm, and agriculture was the chief subject in the curriculum. Selected graduates were sent for a postgraduate year on the trial farm, free of cost, and returned to their villages with the necessary seeds and tools.

The farm and laboratory had been bombed out during the war. Judging from what we had seen of American failure to rebuild, we were prepared to find nothing but ruins and weeds in Hoshino's prize farm.

But the farm had been rejuvenated. It abounded in experiments that might have surprised even the Japanese. New varieties of breadfruit had been introduced that should bear during the months when the Ponape variety does not, thus providing ripe breadfruit all the year round. This is important because, in much of Micronesia, the bread that grows on trees is the staff of life.

Citrus of many kinds was being encouraged, and tropical fruit trees of the cherry and berry families. Other equator-loving introductions were the macadamia nut, rambutan (like lichee), guava, loquat, lanzone of the Philippines, Tahitian chestnut, Malabar chestnut, governor's plum, mountain apple, Mexican apple, star apple—and none of these apples are apples!

A special delight was the mangosteen which Southeast Asia justly calls the "queen of fruits," as delicious as the "king of fruits," the durian, with the added advantage that you don't have to hold your nose.

Naturally not all the experiments were successful. We congratulated Leo on some fine-looking plantings of Kona coffee, but he objected:

"A coffee borer gets into it. It's a small worm; larva of a beetle. Doubtless good nutritious protein, but it rather spoils the taste when you realize that you are imbibing essence of worms with your coffee. But I think we're finding a way to get rid of it."

These foods were for local consumption. Later in a Ponape thatch-roofed farmhouse we sat on handwoven floor mats, surrounded by household articles hardly changed in three hundred years, and were served foods unknown in Ponape a few years ago.

"From our own farm," said the housewife. "We got the seedlings from Ag. Our meals used to be about the same day after day. Now we have many different things. That pleases the children especially. They eat more. It's good for them."

Besides foods for local use, Ponape also needed something to sell abroad, for the Trust's imports were nearly double the exports.

The chief and only significant export was copra, dried meat of the coconut.

But Ag was acclimatizing black pepper, training the vines to climb posts made of the trunks of tree ferns—for the fern, so lowly in northern lands, grows to a height of twenty feet in well-watered South Sea islands. Here was something the island farmer could raise with little or no trouble and the pepper berries find a ready market abroad.

One of the many other export products was cacao (cocoa).

"All the farmers want it," said Leo. "We can't raise enough of the seedlings to meet the demand. There are now 110,000 cacao trees on Ponape. Ponape sold a thousand pounds to the United States last year, it will be three thousand this year, next year six thousand, and can be expected to increase at that rate for years."

11

The Lake in the Sea

IN the fairy islands of Truk we found District Agriculturist George Davis equally enthusiastic about cocoa.

"Only a few years ago the Trukese knew nothing about it, and cared less. Now they are keen about it. The tree is easily raised, produces within three years, and the beans bring a good price—just now fifty-five cents a pound as against only five and a half cents a pound for copra. There is such a demand for seedlings that we expect there will be two million trees producing in Truk by 1970. Then it will be Truk's principal export."

"Displacing copra?"

"Better say, supplementing copra—because that's going to go up, too. We're distributing sixty thousand coconut seedlings a year. The cocoa trees can be planted in among the coconut trees and they help each other. The thick cocoa foliage shades the ground, keeps down grass and weeds, and makes it easy to collect the coconuts. Cocoa leaves make a good mulch. We don't have the coconut beetle here. It's true we have plenty of coconut crabs and they do a lot of damage. Fruit bats eat the coconuts. By the way, the Saipanese eat this bat and since the bat has fed only on sweet fruits, they cook it as it is, without removing the contents of the stomach. But in spite of crabs and bats, copra production climbs every year. We have thirteen extension agents in the Truk islands and they show the people how to dig the holes and how to fertilize. Believe it or not, they've even planted coconuts in the cement airstrip on Eten."

That sounded like a tall story, but we later sailed by the small island of Eten and found the story true. A quarter century before we had seen the Japanese leveling the long, narrow island of Eten and laying a cement airstrip in preparation for the war that they already foresaw. Now Truk farmers have made holes in the cement and planted five thousand coconut palms which grow all the better because the cement around them keeps down the weeds.

Truk lagoon is one of the marvels of the ocean world. It will someday be a famous tourist resort.

Before we first visited Truk we had supposed it to be an island. Instead, it is a constellation of more than two hundred islands and islets in a rainbow-floored lagoon girdled by a coral reef. This encircling reef is 140 miles long. Four gaps allow entrance to the lagoon. Ocean billows spend their force upon the reef, leaving the waters inside as quiet as those of a lake.

This lake in the sea is some forty miles in diameter. Its bottom is at some places very deep, suitable for large ships, but in many reaches the bottom is only fifteen feet down and the coral wonders of the lagoon floor are plainly visible as you look over the rail of a scudding sailboat or motorboat.

The islands within the atoll rise several hundred feet high, clothed from sand beach to summit in coconut palms, banana and breadfruit trees, richly flowering bougainvillea, and hibiscus; and on their crests are the remains of the Japanese gun emplacements which persuaded Nimitz and MacArthur to bypass Truk. The entire District of Truk, extending beyond

Truk itself, is the home of twenty-two thousand Micronesians.

Flying fish and porpoises broke the mirror-smooth surface as we sailed across the lagoon to Tol, largest island in the atoll. Davis was with us, also a very special guest from Washington, Richard Taitano, Director of the Office of Territories, Department of the Interior.

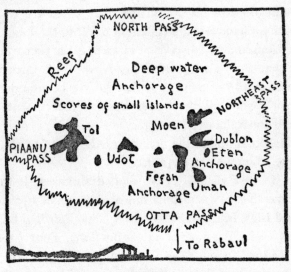

TRUK

In a deep bay we landed to walk through extensive groves of coconut and cacao supplied by Davis and planted by ambitious native farmers. There was every evidence that the farmers and their wives had been hard at work in the groves. It didn't conform with the popular picture of the South Sea islander drowsing under a tree waiting for the fruit to drop.

"That's what makes me so mad," Davis said. "People saying these people are lazy."

But on this particular day the groves were deserted. We soon learned the reason. Entering a jungle-girt farmhouse we found the men of the family busily grating breadfruit, wringing out milk from the white meat of coconuts, and preparing fish and pork for baking in a huge missionary-size pot. They stopped work to talk.

"Where are the ladies?" we inquired of the head of the family.

"Playing bingo."

"Where did they learn that?"

"From your Navy men."

"But you men seem to be doing the cooking."

"Of course. This is Saturday."

The explanation seemed a little obscure. Davis came to the rescue.

"It's the custom," he said. "On Truk the men do the cooking. They do it all on Saturday—enough to last all week. While they cook, the women take a holiday. Come—you'll see how they spend it."

A half mile farther we began to hear the lively chatter of a score of female voices. Emerging into a clearing, we came upon a sort of pavilion, open-sided, palm-roofed, filled with happy women playing bingo. But we were assured they do more serious things as well. They constitute an informal women's club and discuss such matters as infant care, diet, schooling, farming, and the proper training of husbands.

Davis led us on at a terrific pace along an atrocious path full of boulders and mudholes. Why such speed?

I suspected that he had an ulterior motive. Taitano is a small, short-legged man, and no athlete. Davis seemed determined to leave him behind. The agriculturist had already spoken bitterly about the serious need for good roads so that farmers could get their products down to the shipping point. Good roads cost money, and the money must be appropriated in Washington, for such improvements are beyond the means of small local farmers. If Taitano could be impressed, perhaps In-terior could impress Congress.

But the slightly built official, who looked as if he would be most at home with his knees under a desk, kept up with the acrobatic Davis, leaping over stones, logs, and holes with re-markable agility. After three miles of this hop-skip-and-jump, Davis stopped, panting, and I puffed to a halt beside him. Tai-tano was not even breathing hard. He seemed completely un-impressed, and Davis was plainly disappointed.

But, on the sail back to the island of Moen, district head-quarters, the little man from Washington suddenly broke the silence with:

"You know, your worst bottleneck on all these islands is poor transportation."

12.

The Rust Territory

IT is painfully true. Not once in our weeks in the islands after leaving Saipan did we set foot on a pavement—except on Dublon where we walked down the Japanese-made paved street of the former Japanese town.

But now there is no town. Only the bombed-out fragments remain, jagged fragments of walls, colorful tiles from demolished roofs, stairs leading nowhere. We felt the presence of ghosts. It was more forlorn than Goldsmith's deserted village.

What had been the Japanese equivalent of Main Street was now a jungle of weeds, vines, banana trees, breadfruit, palms, mangoes, pressing in so far over the pavement that they almost closed over what had once been a busy thoroughfare. But the concrete was still there as a reproach to postwar road builders who seemed to have forgotten its use.

There was of course good reason for the demolition of Dublon. The vast lagoon of Truk had been the most redoubtable Japanese naval and air base in the Pacific and Dublon had been the headquarters island on which were quartered forty thousand Japanese troops. Truk was bombed, but never taken. It defied the strategists. It was cheaper to go around it than through it. However, Dublon was so thoroughly wrecked that American headquarters were set up on the neighboring island of Moen.

The U.S. Navy had a free field on Moen. They could build freshly, efficiently, imaginatively, in the best American tradition. It was a job worth doing well, for there was not one of the two thousand islands of Micronesia more important strategically than Truk. And the Navy had the money to do the job right. Focus of the entire project was the Administrative Center.

We looked down on it from our hotel window. It consisted of a crossroads of dust (or mud in bad weather), strewn with fist-size rocks. The contrast was striking—on Dublon, the Japanese concrete pavement; here, tire-ruining rubble. Traffic was heavy, since this was the heart of the entire area.

Around this crossroads were grouped, or rather flung, the Administration Building, the hotel, and the hospital, all of sheet iron and resembling cow barns, except that no modern cow barn would be so poorly ventilated. The iron roofs with completely closed gables made the structures perfect bake ovens.

As for the hotel, it stood high on a hillside where it should receive all the benefit of the trade wind. But unhappily it had been so oriented that the northeast trade during the summer months could not enter the rooms on one side, and the rooms on the other side were blocked off from the breeze by an ell containing the kitchen.

Besides the cow barns, there were quonsets, like huge tin cans cut in half, housing the intermediate school, commissary, bank, office of the Truk Congress, the Land Office, the Post Office, Public Health Department, and so forth.

Even the Courthouse, always a matter of architectural pride in an American town, was a quonset.

Naturally the quonset, being essentially a curved iron roof coming to the ground on both sides, is, though doubtless ideal at the South Pole, "hell on earth" in the tropics. The words in quotes represented the sentiment of a man who must hold court in this tin-can Hall of Justice. We slipped into a rear seat of the bake oven to watch him at work. Judge E. P. Furber could hardly appear in a comfortable loincloth. The dignity of his office required that he wear the complete judicial panoply: white shirt, necktie (the only necktie we saw in the entire Trust Territory), coat, and black robe. Of course there was no air conditioning—only one feeble fan. He continually mopped the streams trickling down his face, meanwhile trying to keep his mind on incoherent native testimony, relayed to him through an interpreter who had a very inadequate knowledge of English.

His two court reporters told us that the judge had unending patience in exploring every angle of a case and reaching a fair decision. He had grown old in the service, was a big man, clear-voiced, firm, but never sharp, and evidently held in the highest respect. That he should be subjected to such working conditions was hardly short of criminal.

We went next door to the intermediate school, also housed in quonsets. The school was supposed to be coeducational, but few girls were to be seen. The teacher gave us the reason.

"Parents don't want their girls to become pregnant."

English was being taught, after a fashion. The English of the Micronesian teachers was scarcely better than that of the students. We could not understand the language of either, but did manage to make something of the lesson plan a teacher had taped to the wall:

For 3th Gread

8.30-9—Arith
9-9.30—English
9.30-10—Writing
10-10.30—Long resses
10.30-11.00—Reating
11.00-11.30—Social studies

Students were languid, sleepy, indifferent. It was difficult to imagine how they could be otherwise under the close-fitting roof beneath a tropic sun.

A new school building was going up. We went to inspect it. The dining hall was already constructed and in use. A wave of heat struck us as we went in. There were large glass windows but few of them could be opened. The roof was of corrugated iron and there was no ceiling. Quite evidently it had not been designed by any architect with the slightest knowledge of tropical weather.

Mr. Goding, the new Hicom, was disheartened when, after wading through the mud of what was supposed to be a road, he came within sight of a school on the island of Tol.

"It was a decrepit building with no screens, a dirt floor and a leaky tin roof. I felt like weeping."

His second in command, José Benitez, when taken to visit a similar school, exploded. "This is not a school! This is not America!" And he delivered such a furious kick to the quivering tin walls that the ramshackle edifice nearly collapsed.

Viewed from the hotel, the iron roofs of public buildings were a symphony of different shades of brown according to the degree of rust. Over the rust waved the flags of the UN and the United States. "The rust territory," muttered a guest at our side.

Nothing so spoils the beauty of the tropics as rusty, patched,

corrugated iron roofs. We had made mention of this to Eleanor
Wilson, skipper of the *Morning Star*, upon viewing the sheet-
iron hovels of Majuro.

"It's partly the fault of the trading companies," she said.
"They don't bring in lumber or paint."

"But could the people buy it if it were available?"

"Oh yes. Whenever they stock any of it, it goes like that"—
with a snap of her fingers.

New York Times foreign correspondent Robert Trumbull,
confronting the proudest structures of Truk, commented:

> Clearly, there was no discernible concern for neatness on
> the outside of the administration buildings. There was not
> even the minimum effort toward upkeep that the average
> American would expend on his own home in the United
> States.
>
> Grass went uncut, buildings unpainted, needed repairs
> ignored. For example, I noted the broken screening on the
> main door of the hospital at one district center. The rusted
> wire mesh flapped outward in a large rent, letting in flies and
> mosquitoes. At home, it occurred to me, no American would
> tolerate this. Here, no one seemed to notice.

The saddest result of all this is the effect upon the Trukese.
The example is hardly inspiring. While native houses on remote islands are attractive, those of the shantytowns that hug
the American center reflect what is supposed to be American
taste. The only difference is that the shacks are smaller and the
rust is deeper. Where the rust has eaten completely through
the roof, pieces of tin made from flattened beer cans cover the
holes. Boards and scraps of metal patch the walls. About the
house the earth is bare, and any flower or shrub that dares to
raise its head above the surface is immediately yanked out by
the roots.

A corrugated iron roof shows rust within the year. It thoroughly rusts through in eight years. It takes no mathematical

genius to deduce from these figures that the roof is an eyesore seven-eighths of the time.

And it is so hot that on the island of Rongelap where a benevolent administration built rows of iron-roofed houses on stilts, the occupants found the houses so intolerable that they moved *under* them and lived on the cool earth between the stilts.

In Kapingamarangi Village on Ponape we found the people still clinging obstinately to their traditional architecture. The graceful, high-roofed buildings with steep eaves were beautiful, the heavy thatch roofs excluded the heat, and the woven pandanus walls freely admitted air.

"Why thatch?" we asked the magistrate. "Doesn't it wear out quickly?"

"A thatch roof lasts four or five years," he replied. "Then it can be replaced without expense. The materials are right here, all around us. It's cool. And we think it's attractive."

It is attractive. And an attractive house preserves morale. Those who live in it are proud of it, keep it looking nice, and improve the surroundings.

If you don't believe it, visit Samoa. The loveliest native houses of the Pacific are to be found there. Every house is a jewel, and just as a jewel requires a beautiful setting, the charm of the Samoan house stimulates those who live in it to cultivate a lovely garden. The Samoans actually organize garden clubs. Competitions are held and prizes awarded for the best gardens. It's only human nature. A good home inspires good care.

A visitor from the UN deploring the tin huts of Truk in the vicinity of the metalized administration buildings was told:

"You can't stop the people from imitating Western architecture."

The answer to this argument is of course that the iron-roof

monstrosities of the administrative center do not even faintly represent Western architecture.

The way to disillusion islanders who suppose these rustbacks to be Western is to put up buildings that are really Western. This applies not only to the public buildings but to the homes of American personnel. Why not engage a good architect to design houses that will combine native style with Western convenience?

And why not take delegations of Micronesian leaders and particularly builders to Samoa to see what a prideful home can be built of native materials?

And how about erecting a "model home" as a demonstration of what can be done with materials ready at hand?

And produce a motion picture of beautiful native homes in other parts of the Pacific. Send it on tour through the islands.

Don't tell me these people can't be led. They've already been misled. If they can be misled they can be led.

To get back to roads.

The observation of the little man from Washington, "Your worst bottleneck on these islands is poor transportation," is exemplified in Ponape. The Japanese had a road all the way around this great island. Now we had found it overgrown and impassable.

Only broken fragments remained of the pavement that once stretched two miles down the principal street of Koror on Palau.

We were to find only dirt roads on Yap, even in the sizable town of Colonia. Outside of town, Yap was a pothole paradise. The cars were as bad as the slipped-disc roads. Riding in an antiquated jeep to the southern end of the island we followed ruts eighteen inches deep punctuated by sudden pitfalls still deeper. On the way back to town the foot brake gave out completely and upon trying the hand brake it was found to be useless. So we jolted ten miles up and down fairly steep and twisting grades, brakeless!

The Distad informed us that he had had six flat tires in the last ten days. A Public Works official put it this way:

"What we have out here is low-level maintenance of second-hand equipment."

The net result is of course that people move as little as possible. Normal communication and commerce are severely handicapped.

The UN Trusteeship Council keeps harping upon "the close link which exists between economic expansion and the development of transport facilities, including inter-island air and sea transport as well as surface transport in some of the larger islands for the more economical transport of crops."

The Administration is keenly aware of this situation. But it has not been financially able to do much about it. Truk reported to the visiting UN Mission:

"Shipping service outside the lagoon to outer islands of the district continues to be irregular and quite unpredictable due to engine and mechanical failure on the field-trip vessel and the recurring need to divert the vessel for temporary service elsewhere. There is limited incentive to increase quality or quantity of copra when out-islanders experience long intervals between shipping, and resultant copra spoilage."

Until surface roads, air roads, ship roads, can fill the need, not only roofs will rust but the whole island economy, and the people as well.

13.

The Truk Tahiti

ANY man-made ugliness on Truk is the more noticeable because of the magnificence of the natural surroundings.

"To my mind Truk is the most beautiful of the island groups of Micronesia"—so writes explorer James Ramsey Ullman in his delicious book, *Where the Bong Tree Grows*. Early Spanish explorers went even further. They reported it "the loveliest cluster of islands in the Pacific."

If I should be reliably informed that heaven was closed to me but were allowed to choose any other spot in which to spend eternity, I should think twice about Truk.

Its name is not musical, but its sea, land and sky are a symphony. Its forty-mile-wide lagoon sheltered by a white girdle of coral is paradise for a yachtsman. There are no disturbing swells and billows, yet always a breeze.

You sail over broad lakes, shoot through narrow passages between islands, skim past sleepy thatched villages on palm-shadowed beaches, drink sunshine, relish the spray, and haul in barracuda over the lee rail.

And below, what a pageant! The lagoon floor is a garden of coral and algae, of sea fan and oarweed, of bright blue sea moss and red sea cucumbers, of ultramarine starfish and of swimming fish in all the colors of the rainbow. There are corals like sponges and sponges like corals. There are green sponges, geranium-scarlet sponges, marigold-yellow sponges.

You get color-dizzy and look back at the plain blue sky for relief.

You put on mask and snorkel and slip into the warm sea.

You float face down over the coral gardens some ten feet below you. It is as if you were in a helicopter, or on a magic carpet. Coral heads rise like palaces and castles pierced by many openings and through these portals fish wearing costumes as colorful as those of the knights and ladies of old pass in and out.

But no castles and palaces were ever so colorful. Many of the colors are new to you, colors not seen in the land world, colors you can't name.

There is staghorn coral like a submarine tree, but a tree made up of minute living animals. There is brain coral, round-headed, and seamed with the convolutions that give it its name. There is the black-spined sea urchin and the white-spined sea porcupine. And if your foot or your hand touches these needles you will be in trouble for weeks. A flower with hundreds of petals draws them in as your shadow passes over it—for they are the tentacles of the sea anemone which snare unsuspecting fishes and pass them in through the always-hungry mouth.

There are giddily colored angelfish, butterfly fish, parrot fish and unnamable pink fish, blue fish, brown fish, together with multitudes of brilliant tiny yellow fish that swim up to your face plate and gaze in as curiously as you gaze at them.

The bottom suddenly drops away and you feel that you are about to fall from the edge of the precipice to unfathomable depths. For you are now in one of the great anchorages that at times accommodated the entire Japanese fleet.

You return to the deck of your boat and look out over this remarkable pastel-green lake set down in an indigo ocean. The white ribbon of reef that surrounds the lake is some hundreds of feet wide, but broadens in places to form islands with perfect sand beaches and shady parklike groves of coconut palms. No one of these islands is as high as the deck from which you view it.

The necklace on which these beads are strung is one hundred and forty miles in length. Within it there is no blank sheet of water as in many atolls of the Marshalls. Instead there is a fantasia reminding one of a Chinese painting. Quite improbable mountains tower like tipsy minarets to heights of a thousand feet and more.

They contrast oddly with the flat ruglike islands of the rim; for while these are coral, the inner islands are volcanic and still suggest the violence that formed them.

Not only their shape, but their number seems improbable. Besides ten sizable islands there are scores of entrancing islets, their tropic colors contrasting with the white sails of fishing boats.

It seems much too charming to have been Japan's grimmest sea base. But a tiger is beautiful, too.

Even the quite ungeological layman wonders how this amazing galaxy of islands, tall and flat, was formed. The explanation seems to be that there once towered here a single great volcano. Streams cut the mass into many separate mountains. Then the land subsided, leaving only the tops of the mountains above water—and these mountaintops are the two hundred and forty-five islands of Truk.

The great volcano had been bordered by the usual fringing reef. As the land sank, water separated the reef from the land, forming the present lagoon. Of course the reef sank too, but the polyps were still busily at work and built new coral on top of the old, thus keeping the height of the reef constant. The result is a rim of coral with an outer cliff dropping to a depth of three miles. Within the lagoon the depth varies from ten feet to several hundred.

You sail on through a flaming sunset. Darkness creeps up the mountains until only the pinnacles are lit. Then they too go black and it is night.

But an imposssibly beautiful night. The moon is full, and a full moon in the South Seas is the richest gift of the sky to man. You could read small type with ease, but who wants to read small type on a night like this? The deck is bathed in milk. The jib and mainsail float above like smoke. Orion blazes overhead, trailing brilliant Sirius. They show off to as great advantage as gems laid out on a pad of blue velvet on a jeweler's showcase. At one end of the sky is the North Star and at the other end will soon rise the Southern Cross. The horizon is cushioned with white puffballs of clouds, their crests snowy in the moonlight. The bow waves sparkle like fountains. The coral colors of the lagoon floor melt liquidly one into another. We flow along with amazing speed, for the wind, though gentle, is abaft the beam. Our half-clothed native friends, perched, singing, on the weather rail, look like statues of marble and bronze combined.

On a peak of Dublon rise the dark ruins of what was once the Japanese governor's official residence. How well I remember that spot!

We had wondered how to get ashore on Truk. It would probably be more difficult than elsewhere because of the strategic importance of this Japanese base.

But the problem solved itself. Shortly after the ship cast anchor in the lagoon a handsome Polynesian climbed aboard. He stopped short when he saw a white man, then came to me, all smiles.

"You are American?" he asked eagerly. "'For twenty years I have not seen an American. My name is Fal. I used to be a chief —now no more. There was an American missionary here. His name was Logan. That was long ago, before the yellows came. He was a father to me. He taught me English. He was good to my people. I swore I would do anything for an American. You will come to my home?"

"If you can get us off quietly," I said. "The captain wouldn't want us to land."

He looked around. "Everybody is up forward. Go aft. I'll have my boat there. It has a little cabin. Slip into the cabin and no one will know you are aboard."

In ten minutes we were flying toward shore in Fal's big outrigger sailing canoe.

"Take us straight to the governor," I said to Fal. The best way to flout authority is to pretend to respect it. It wouldn't do to wait for police to pick us up and take us before the governor of the island. We had best go to him under our own power and present our credentials.

We avoided the docks and landed on a quiet beach on Dublon. Above us towered a hill crowned by a building in German style. It had been the residence of the German governor and was now occupied by his Japanese successor.

We climbed up, called a polite "*Ohaiyo*," the Japanese equivalent of a knock on the door, were admitted by a bewildered attendant and met the much-astonished Governor Yamaguchi. After the first "*Sa!*" he covered his surprise well. He expressed great pleasure that we should consider his poor islands worth visiting.

"I am afraid you will be disappointed," he said. "There is nothing of interest here."

Tea was brought in, and we talked. Suddenly there came a blast from the harbor.

"Your ship!" exclaimed the governor. "It is sailing!"

"It is just going to Kusaie," I said, "and will be back in a week."

"A week!" he gasped.

But there was nothing for it. We were Truk's unwelcome guests for a week.

I came near staying there forever at the bottom of the Truk lagoon.

We were assigned to Fal's care and lived in his log-and-thatch home. Fal stood in well with the Japanese. They had made him a *soncho* or administrator over several dozen villages. The Japanese trusted Fal—as much as they trust anyone. They did not dream what was in his heart.

"The Americans will come back someday," he said. "Until then we can only obey."

Fal took us on endless trips among the myriad islands. Sometimes we went shark hunting just inside the lagoon. Everywhere we were followed at a distance by a police boat. I do not doubt that a complete dossier of my movements lay before the governor. When I saw him his cordiality was more extravagant and less sincere than ever. I told him of our shark-hunting trips.

"I am so glad you are enjoying our islands," he said.

A day later Fal took me aside where we could not be overheard. "They kill me if they know I tell you this," he said. "They want me to take you sharking again."

"I have no objection to that!"

"But they tell me not to bring you back."

The canoe was to upset, he told me, and I was to be most unfortunately drowned. It was all very simple, from the Japanese viewpoint.

Fal could not refuse. That would immediately convict him of complicity with a foreign spy. He must make at least a good show of trying to lose me.

We laid a plan by which I should escape drowning by a sufficiently narrow margin to convince the authorities that Fal had done his best. But if the plan slipped a little and the drowning happened to be too thorough . . . ? It was with a tingling spinal sensation that I set out with Fal on this strange errand.

We harpooned a shark at last. Standing in the canoe, the better to manipulate the line, we were wrenched in a wild, tipsy zigzag across the lagoon.

Half a mile away was the usual police boat. Binoculars were trained upon us. We waited until we came within swimming distance of Dublon Island.

"Now!" said Fal, as the boat twisted.

I fell overboard. It was plain to the eyes behind the binoculars that Fal could have cut the line and returned to save me. He did not. I called after him and stretched out an appealing arm, but in vain.

Thrashing violently to keep off sharks, I started toward shore. It was slow work, for I am not a good swimmer. More than once I wondered if we had not made our little act a bit too realistic. Gray shapes scudded by. At last I stood on the beach.

I went to the governor that evening and complained of Fal's negligence. The governor seemed much distressed. "I shall see that the kanaka is properly punished," he said and promptly wrote out an order, presumably for the police.

The police did come to see Fal; when they left he told me they had complimented him on his effort and instructed him to try again.

But our ship came the next day.

It is now safe to tell of Fal's trick upon his Japanese masters, for he is secure in the Polynesian heaven. He escaped from the Micronesian islands to the Solomons, where American boys reported him and other brown chiefs fighting at their side. He fell fighting.

Now for the first time since the Spaniards landed on its shores, Truk is freely open to visitors—and will be until and unless new wars make necessary its reconversion into a military base. Hotel accommodations are being greatly improved, facilities for seeing the wonders of the atoll are being provided. Here is a new Tahiti.

Nothing can replace the old Tahiti. But Truk has features that Tahiti lacks. There is the great enclosed lagoon. There are scores of small islands instead of a single great island. A good hundred of these islands are uninhabited; so you may, if you wish, enjoy the sensation of having an island all to yourself. There is fine sailing and fine fishing. There has not been enough skin diving to make fish spear-conscious. There is none of the crowding that makes Waikiki and now Papeete a bit breathless. There is the charm of the unknown. Away from the administrative center and its shantytowns there are simple people with smiling manners and uncommercialized hospitality. May they not be spoiled by the cruise ships that must soon be calling at Truk.

14

Backward, Turn Backward

THE Albatross settled on the lagoon of Palau, that superb fling of two hundred islands in a chain 125 miles long protected from the violence of ocean by a barrier reef.

The Japanese had prized it so much that they had made its chief town, Koror, their capital for the administration of all Micronesia.

"You'll see some changes," said Distad Francis Mahoney, slipping behind the wheel of the jeep, "and I'm afraid they aren't all for the better."

Changes indeed. We drove up the main street. It had been concrete. Now it was dirt. Clouds of dust enveloped us. The jeep bumped and bucked over loose chunks of the former pavement.

The street had been solidly lined for two miles by government buildings, department stores, shops, studios, fine residences, radio towers, schools, steamship offices, bookstores, neon-lit cafés, Shinto shrines, Buddhist temples, Christian churches, theaters, and geisha houses. Now it had largely reverted to jungle. It was before the war a town of twenty thousand people, fifty thousand after the Japanese troops moved in.

Now, said the Distad, the population was under four thousand.

We saw forlorn remains of past glory—tumbled gateposts, stone lanterns, sculptured lions, memorial tablets, half covered by weeds and vines. From the crumbled mass casuarina trees had sprung up.

The best building the town afforded was Japanese. Well designed and strongly built, it had escaped the bombs. Formerly it had been the telephone exchange. Now that the population had declined and with it the telephone service, the building housed the Administration. Ironical, that after nearly two decades of American occupation of Palau a Japanese building should remain the only fit structure for the officers of the U.S. government!

We drew up before the hotel. It appeared too modest to bear so proud a name—the Royal Palauan.

"The Navy boys built it and gave it its name," said Mahoney, "because it was far from royal. But it's been improved since. Now it almost deserves the name. Anyhow, it's the best in the Trust Territory."

We were assigned the "royal suite," consisting of sitting room, bedroom, bath and two hot lockers. The hot locker is a luxury that is almost a necessity in this humid climate. The windows gave on pleasant gardens of tropical plants and trees— ti, banana, and casuarina. The public rooms of the hotel were comfortable, the food good. The building was being extended to accommodate the expected increase in visitors. A travel agency had been formed, and provision made for special tours, deep-sea fishing, camping, hiking, skin diving, boating, and the unique entertainment afforded by Palauan dancers and musicians.

Palau had been the Miami Beach of wealthy Japanese who fled the winter of Japan to bask in the tropics, preferring Palau because of its natural beauty and the liveliness and luxury of its

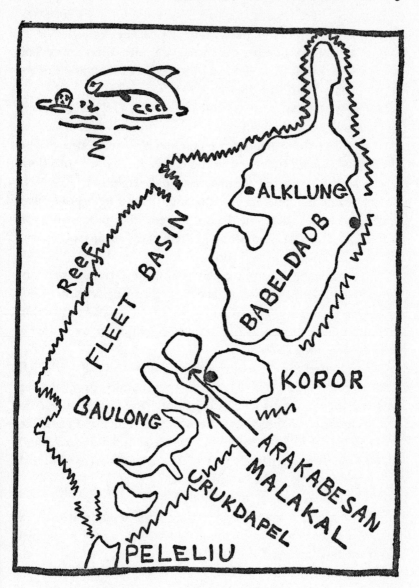

PALAU

capital city. The natural beauty is still there, and efforts are being made to regenerate the liveliness if not the luxury.

At least the visitor may now enjoy the pleasant sensation of being heartily welcomed instead of feeling that he is at all times under a heavy cloud of suspicion.

Not that the Japanese were discourteous. On the contrary, they were almost too good to us. Wherever we went, a shadow came slipping along behind us. Upon challenge, it turned out to be a policeman, following us, he claimed, for our protection.

The stranger was not permitted to feel neglected. The New Yorker who complains of the difficulty of finding a policeman would have delighted in Palau. There the procedure was simple. Step out of your door, go ten paces in any direction, and lo! a policeman behind you.

The gentleman would be courteous in the extreme, cordially interested in knowing where the foreigner might wish to go, and eager to extend "every facility." His sole mission was to be helpful. I have never in my life been subjected to so much sheer helpfulness.

"They look sharp on white people," remarked a Palau chief.

The white visitor was rare and he generally stopped over only for the hours his ship was in port. An official entertainment committee offered to show him the sights of Palau. He was whirled off to a geisha house, there was much drinking and dancing and the gentle charms of the island Circes detained him until someone looked at his watch.

"Oh! Time to get back to the boat!"

The rare and extraordinary visitor who actually wished to stop over from one boat to the next was grudgingly permitted to do so, but he was the object of unremitting curiosity as to why he should maroon himself here when he didn't have to. Something funny about it. Better keep him provided with every facility.

Two German professors on vacation chose to paddle about in a rubber boat. A government pinnace containing police and sandwiches followed them everywhere lest they should get lost or go hungry. One day they paddled off through a mangrove canal too shallow for the pinnace. They came back at night to find a row of anxious officials seated on their doorstep, and their lack of consideration in causing so much uneasiness to their guardians was brought home to them in no uncertain terms.

An American artist's motor failed and his small boat drifted from Hawaii to Palau. That was indiscreet of it, for he had no landing permit and nothing to show that he had not drifted there by intention. His arrival was the sensation of the island. The motor was repaired but he had no money to pay for the repairs. His request that he be allowed to remain until he could get the money was politely refused. He was given a farewell dinner with speeches. Every facility for his departure was accorded to him and the finest government launch towed him in his motorless boat well outside the reef. He then proceeded to drift, with better judgment this time, to American soil, landing some weeks later in the Philippines. He was later reported to be feverishly painting pictures along the Mindanao coast to earn enough money to retrieve his motor. He held no grudge against the Japanese, in fact considered it all worth while for the thrill of sudden importance he enjoyed on Palau.

The complaint of a German that he had been shadowed reached the Mandates Commission at its meeting in October, 1935. Mr. Ito, the Japanese representative, explained that the traveler in question was tubercular, therefore the Japanese wanted "to take good care of him." It was quite probable, Mr. Ito suggested, that this "care" had caused the German "to mistake Japanese hospitality for surveillance."

As for the famous case of Colonel Earl Ellis of the United

States Marines who died mysteriously while investigating conditions on Palau, the Japanese protested indignantly that there was no truth in the rumors that he was "liquidated." Ex-champion Gene Tunney, visiting in Japan, asked about this after my return to Tokyo.

"Nobody knows," I said. "But they say Ellis drank himself to death."

"Pretty hard, don't you think?" said Tunney. "Look at the efforts I've been making all these years!"

Tunney's efforts were not too serious, but it was reported that Ellis broke under the tropic strain and took heavily to the bottle when his boat did not come on time to carry him away. Excess led to fever, it was said, and fever to death. But a less official version is that he was neatly poisoned by the Japanese. Whatever the truth or falsity of conflicting reports, it is at least certain that an American Marine investigating a Japanese island was bound to find himself an unwelcome guest.

A British army officer wearing many medals stopped for a day on his way to New Guinea. He stayed in the German missionary's house . . . and five officials with him. When he stepped into another room, or to the outhouse, he was accompanied. Three officials sat in a row by the edge of the tub as he took a bath. Doubtless they feared he might escape through the drain.

We also, upon arrival, were quartered in the house of the German missionary. Herr Siemer, observing my notebook, warned me that it would be read daily during our absence from the house, His two house boys, though natives, were, he had reason to believe, acting as spies for the police. Sometimes I left the notebook on the bedroom table, sometimes at the bottom of the deepest traveling bag or dresser drawer. Always I found it where I had left it; but not exactly. The slight change of position was just enough to show that it had been removed and replaced.

I was amused one day when the Secretary for Foreign Affairs used a phrase from my notebook, evidently not realizing where he had picked it up. I complimented him on its aptness, and he was pleased.

No information of a geographic or strategic nature went into the notebook. It was preserved in other ways. The pages overflowed with birds, flowers and folkways. Now and then there would be a pleasant word about one or another of the officials who were honoring us with so much attention.

When we had been in Palau for a month the governor said, "You are the only visitors to have thought it worth while to stay with us so long. We have been greatly honored. I am sorry to learn that you are leaving us tomorrow."

We too were sorry to learn that we were leaving, but promptly fell in with the suggestion. Remembering the fate of the U.S. marine who had overstayed his welcome, we sailed on the *Yamashiro Maru* the next morning.

⁂

Why had the Japanese been supersensitive about Palau?

For good reason. This had been expressed by the governor when I asked him why the government for all the Japanese Nanyo had been established on Palau. He mused a moment and then replied, "Palau is near everything that matters."

The samurai sword which slashed so deeply into the southern Pacific had its handle in Japan, its blade in the Marianas and Carolines—and Palau was its fire-hardened point.

Palau was the nearest Japanese outpost to the Philippines. The nearest to Singapore. The nearest to Australia. The nearest to the Netherlands Indies.

There is a Japanese saying, "A drawn sword must taste

blood." After a samurai had once taken his sword from its sheath he was considered an arrant coward if he replaced it unbloodied.

Japan could not resist the temptation to use the sword placed in her hands by the Versailles Conference—the sword tipped with deadly Palau.

When the day came for armed attack upon the Philippines, it sprang from Palau.

The fabulous and coveted islands of Borneo, Celebes, the Moluccas, and New Guinea were attacked from the hundred-mile naval base of the Palau lagoon. The farthest of these, Borneo, was but twelve hundred miles away, bomber-plane range. New Guinea was only six hundred miles distant. The stiff and long resistance of Japanese forces in New Guinea must be largely credited to Palau.

"Palau is the spigot of our oil barrel," remarked an official of the Nanyo.

He did not mean that there was oil in Palau but that Palau was so placed that it could be used to tap the oil riches of the Indies. The Nipponese navy had long been acutely conscious of the importance of Japan's path to the oil lands. Wrote Commander H. Sato in Brassey's *Naval and Shipping Annual:*

> One half of the oil import of Japan is drawn from the Dutch Indies; the freedom of that sea route will be absolutely necessary for her power of resistance.

Directly south of Palau fourteen hundred miles was Australia itself. The Japanese military hoped to see the Palau sword point pierce the "empty continent" where only seven million people held a land larger than continental United States.

Palau is equally important to the United States, though the objectives have changed. Palau is the nearest of the Micronesian bases to troublesome Indonesia, the nearest to harassed Malaysia, the nearest to war-torn Vietnam, dubious Laos and Cambodia, threatened Thailand. It is the nearest to the million-man Red army massed along China's southern border from the Gulf of Tonkin to Kashmir.

Its people are of unusual interest because, of all the Micronesians, they are the nearest to civilization and the nearest to barbarism. The change has been more abrupt than elsewhere. Since Koror was the capital, the metropolis, the cosmopolis of the entire Nanyo, it brought a flood of Japanese unparalleled in any other part of this island world. The relatively modern ideas of the Japanese snapped the Palauans abruptly into the twentieth century.

And yet just under the skin of the older folk was a primitive headhunter. We went to a Christian church service in the village of Ngiwal. The elderly chief was in attendance. He was dressed in his Sunday best—a shirt, but no trousers because the night was warm. He was a bloodthirsty-looking wretch but we were given to understand that he had long ago repented of his record of 280 heads and was now a staunch pillar of the church. He invited us to come to his home the next morning.

We did so. In the uncertain light of the windowless native house, we discerned a few heads on a shelf. He apologized for not having more, but the Japanese, he complained, were zealous collectors of these trophies. He took one down and demonstrated with professional authority how a head should be severed. Drawing his two-foot-long cutlasslike knife from its carved wooden scabbard, he caressed the imaginary neck with the keen blade.

"The blow should come from behind, not in front," he said, illustrating with knife and head. "If you strike in front, your man may protect his neck by lowering his chin; and even if you do reach his neck, the muscles may slow up the blade so that it will not have force enough left to cut the backbone. So you strike from behind, sever the backbone first. The rest doesn't matter. You will have plenty of time to cut the muscles and skin after the man is dead. And notice that the blow should be slanting, not straight."

On the same principle, apparently, as the diagonal stroke of a razor.

"Some white people say we are cowardly because we always attack from behind," went on the king. "It is not so. It is just that we know the right way to do."

Palau headhunting was never conducted for the purpose of displaying courage. The man sent out by his tribe to get a head of the enemy tribe was expected to go about it like a sneak thief. Far from openly challenging anyone to battle, he would lie in wait among the bushes beside the trail and spring out behind a fisherman plodding under a load of nets, or a woman carrying home taro, or a child chasing a butterfly. Upon his return he received the same praise whether the head was that of man, woman, or child.

"What difference did it make?" said the chief. "A child eats as much as a man. There were too many people and too little food on these islands. We made war so that we might eat. If we could stop a young mouth from a lifetime of eating, it was even better than stopping an old one."

But the desperation of hunger paused short of cannibalism. There is no record that human flesh was ever eaten on Palau.

The chief took us to the nearby All Men House. Before it was a circular stone platform called *ailiuth*. At its center was an *olgal*, a stone with a hollow in its upper surface forming a stone cup.

When a "warrior" returned from a successful foray, the head he brought was placed in this cup. Then the tribesmen gathered on the ailiuth and danced about the head, clapping their hands. Toddy made the occasion merrier.

A delegation was organized and sent on a tour of neighboring friendly villages. At each the proud trophy, perhaps the tousled head of some youngster, was placed in the local olgal and became the center of festivities lasting two or three days. The village fed the delegation well, paid it some money for its service in reducing Palau's food problem, and sent it on its way to the next village.

"But I suppose you were especially proud when you got the head of a chief," I said.

"No, no!" The chief was shocked. "That was forbidden. We would kill a chief, but not cut off his head. That would be a disgrace."

Like depriving a general of his sword. So apparently there was some honor even among cutthroats.

He took us through an overgrown path to the grave of the giant of Ngiwal. The story of the giant Ngireumelas is well known among the natives of the Palau Islands and probably has some basis in truth. It seems that about one hundred years ago enemy villages which resented the adeptness of Ngiwal experts in picking off heads united to punish this mischievous village. They killed all the males and decreed that there should never be any more. Thenceforth every man-child born was to be killed.

But one woman who bore a strong son tattooed him as a girl and dressed him as a girl. He grew to great size and, singlehanded, subdued the enemies of Ngiwal. Now he sleeps in a grave so long that when the five-foot chief lay down upon it, touching his toes to the footstone, there was a gap of four feet between his head and the headstone.

The powerful influence of the Japanese upon the Palauans was partly due to the fact that they were blood cousins. The Japanese preferred not to remember that their own blood was partly Micronesian. One of the racial currents in Japanese history came from Malay and Polynesian lands up through the

Micronesian melting pot to Japan, there to blend with the Mongoloid element from Asia.

Many traces of this pilgrimage may be found in Japan. For example, the legends of the Japanese have it that their god, Izanagi, wore a "multitudinous and close-toothed comb in the right bunch of his hair." Exactly such a comb has been worn immemorially by the natives of Yap, whence the custom was probably brought north and practiced by the early barbarians of Japan.

The Japanese only a century ago blacked their teeth and, in fact, the mistress of a *machiai* or waiting house for geisha still does, as a matter of fashion. The Mongols never did this. It is distinctly a Micronesian and Malayan habit. Japanese houses of the early period resembled those of the islands. The influence is still felt and the flimsy Japanese house of today is not nearly so well suited to the rigors of a Japanese winter as to the seasonless climate of the South Seas.

Old Japan followed the odd custom of confining a woman every month and particularly at childbirth in a "parturition house," a one-roomed, windowless hut situated in the forest well away from the villages. Exactly the same custom is practiced to this day in Yap.

Adolescent girls were regularly violated in old Japan in order to test, before marriage, their ability to bear children. The identical custom persists in Yap.

Cannibalism was not practiced in Micronesia but head-hunting was; and in feudal Japan head chopping was a privilege of the samurai.

Also one is struck by the fact that the ancient gods of Japan and the South Seas are similar.

Observing the attitude of the Japanese toward the islander, one would never imagine that they were brothers under the skin.

Currents flowed both ways. Black and brown influence came north, yellow went south. There is more than a trace of Mongol blood in Micronesia and it probably came from Japan.

The Japanese, before their era of seclusion, were great sea rovers and pirates. There have been many authenticated cases of Japanese junks being wrecked in the islands. It is believed that the island of Lele at Kusaie was settled by Japanese. When a Japanese training ship visited Kusaie in 1884 the king told the visitors that his people were descendants of the Japanese race. There are frequent traces of the Japanese languages in the dialects of the islands. There are many similarities in culture.

Long before Japan formally took over the islands, James M. Alexander noted the Japanese strain in Micronesia. He wrote in 1895:

> The Micronesians are a mixed race, part Polynesian and part Japanese with traces of Papuan. The Japanese element is accounted for by the fact that Japanese voyagers have occasionally been storm-driven to great distances over the ocean through the belt of Micronesian islands. In 1814 the British brig, *Forester,* met with a Japanese junk off the coast of California with three living men and fourteen dead bodies on board. In December 1832 a Japanese junk arrived at Hawaii with four of her crew living. The Micronesians are darker and of smaller stature than the Polynesians, but in western Micronesia they are of lighter complexion and more like the Japanese.

There is no such blood affinity between the Americans and the Palauans and the power of numbers is gone. In the latter days of the Japanese occupation there were five Japanese in Palau to every Palauan. Now there is one American to a hundred Palauans. So it is not surprising that there has been a backsliding into old ways. This back eddy does not revive headhunting, but it does give new life to primitive techniques and ancient superstitions. It leaves stranded many young people who abandoned old taboos for the new, and now are abandoned by the new.

One result is juvenile delinquency, a sore problem today in Palau. To combat it a Youth Corps has been organized "to utilize the labor of young men for purposeful community enterprise such as road rehabilitation, clearing land, improvement of docks and waterways."

This sounds encouraging—until we note that the Corps is operating on only two islands. There are two hundred islands in the Palau group.

※

On some of the out islands the only persons combating juvenile delinquency may be the missionaries. These are sometimes picturesque and appealing characters.

Take the priest of Ngaraard, four hours by motorboat from Koror. It was low tide when we arrived, so we had to wade a quarter mile to shore, pushing the boat, then walk half a mile up the beach to the mission of Father Edwin McManus, a spirited little Irish-Italian, bearded, articulate, well informed and not too otherworldly—in fact we had been advised to take him a bottle of Scotch, and did so.

His small house was half full of bags of Portland cement and stacks of plywood sheets to be used as ceiling in the church he was building.

His home bore no trace that a woman had ever passed through it. The floor was uncovered cement, the walls and ceiling unpainted, the kitchen and shower facilities primitive, and the *benjo* was a separate institution reached by a woodland path.

There were no electric lights, no refrigerator, no radio, no phonograph, no water heater, no hot locker, no glass windows, no screens on windows or doors, no easy chair.

"Why live so simply?" we asked. "Surely you don't need to."

"My neighbors live simply," he replied. "I'd lose my influence with them if I put on airs. Really, I haven't much choice. The mission society leaves me pretty much on my own. But it isn't too bad. My neighbors bring me fruit and taro. Every six months I order a shipment of canned goods from the United States. It gets here three months later."

A sheet was strung up across the room as a curtain and we slept behind it on army cots. In the morning he took us to his school in a new building that he had laid block by block with his own hands. Here elementary education and Catholic doctrine were dispensed to seventy girls and boys.

"And you'll want to see my Protestant friends." We walked a few hundred feet down the trail to the home of the sisters who conduct a Protestant Liebenzeller (Swiss) Mission and girls' intermediate school with eighty students.

Only one of the three *Schwestern* was there, this being vacation. Miss Thiem had the floor littered with Bibles and manuscripts—she was translating the Bible into Palauan and was up to Colossians. The father himself was compiling a Palauan-English dictionary.

"Funny language," he said. "There are so many ideas you simply can't express in Palauan. It has only about six thousand words—we have six hundred thousand in English. There are only about half as many letters in the alphabet as in English. For example, there's no V or F in Palauan. B is used instead. A Palauan father proudly told me he had given all his three sons names beginning with B—Bernard, Bincent and Brancis."

He mused for a moment. Then he said, "Sometimes I wonder if it's worthwhile. I mean this dictionary, and translating the Bible." Sister Thiem looked shocked. "I mean," he went on, "all this devotion to a poor language. It can never be as useful as a world language, like English. It's impossible to print

textbooks in all the languages and dialects of the Trust Territory. Perhaps we ought to concentrate on teaching English. Of
course we do teach it, but not enough. Even a ninth-grade student can't read English intelligently. The Japanese taught Japanese far better than English is being taught now."

"How about religion?" we asked. "Do the people accept it?"

"In a way, yes. But old superstitions persist. For example,
people around here are afraid of spirits. They wouldn't think
of walking alone at night. They ask me, 'Aren't you afraid to
live alone?' A Palauan left alone would move in with neighbors."

Superstition had a new lease on life when Japan drove out
the missionaries and kept them out for five years, 1917-21. The
purpose was to leave the field free for the Japanese doctrines of
Buddhism and Shintoism.

The result was not as expected. The Palauans did not take to
the Japanese faiths. Nor did they revert completely to old beliefs. Instead, they invented a religion of their own.

It was a weird medley of ideas picked up from Catholic and
Protestant theology together with some persisting features of
the old nature worship and ancestor worship. But the chief in-
gredient, and the most annoying to the Japanese, was a spirit of
nationalism, a drive for independence. It was a form of the
"cargo cult" that had for years been spreading through the
South Pacific, and is still very much alive—the fantastic notion
that the day is at hand when cargo ships will appear over the
horizon loaded with all the good things of the Western world,
automobiles, refrigerators, TV, electric stoves, air conditioners,
and unlimited funds to be distributed free of charge to every
islander, brown or black. At the same time the foreigners, white
or yellow, will leave the islands never to return.

This doctrine was hardly acceptable to the Japanese and they
did their best to suppress it. Like most religions, it thrived on

persecution. It continued to spread. The clever Japanese saw their mistake, quit the policy of suppression, and set about reviving Christianity. But with this difference: the missionaries now brought into the islands were Japanese.

There is, of course, a strong native Christian church in Japan. This church has for many years been sending out its own missionaries, Japanese, to carry the Cross to other lands. Japan is not so unreservedly Buddhist or Shinto as the Western world imagines. The supposedly "pagan" Japanese government has for many years been subsidizing Protestant and Catholic missions in lands it controls or hopes to control. It is to be doubted that Japanese officials hold a prayer meeting when sending their yen forth to evangelize the world. In fact it is a sufficiently hard-boiled procedure activated by the conviction that religion, and especially Christianity, is "good for" the natives. It makes them "easy to govern." It helps to make them meek and pliable.

Religion can more easily be made a tool of national policy if it is operated by representatives of the nation, not by aliens.

On Truk we had met the Reverend Kawashima, serving under the *Nanyo Dendo-dan* or South Sea Mission financed by the Japanese government.

"But doesn't the government support Shinto priests in the islands?" I asked the missionary.

"Very few. Shinto is a warlike faith. Shinto may do for the Japanese, but not for these people. It would lead them astray. Not that I have anything against Shinto. I am a Shintoist."

"You are both a Christian and a Shintoist?"

"Of course. Why not?"

"You don't find any conflict between the conception of a Christian God and the conception of a God-Emperor?"

"Not at all. The Christian God in the form of Christ was a great prophet and we deeply honor him. He was an Oriental, crucified by the West but accepted by us of the East. There is a tradition, you know, that he came to Japan and honored the *Tenshi* [Emperor] as his father and father of all mankind. It is said that he died in Japan and is buried there. But God still lives."

"By 'God' you mean the Emperor?"

Mr. Kawashima smiled at my crudeness. "I can hardly explain to one not brought up in the same religious atmosphere. No, we do not think of the reigning Emperor as God. What we revere is the Godhead which began with the Creator, Izanagi, continued in Amaterasu, the Sun Goddess, and her grandson, the first Emperor, Jimmu, and flowed through all his imperial successors to the present day."

It was an odd kind of Christianity. Its influence upon the Micronesians died out soon after the Japanese left. But the Palauan cult, called Modekngei, is now the religion of one Palauan in every three. American officials do not encourage it by suppression. They ignore it, believing it will break down in the face of better education and self-government.

The few dozen Americans in Palau, a mere handful compared with the Japanese who sometimes numbered fifty thousand, are doing what they can to build more schools, train more Palauan teachers, bring in more American teachers to work with their Palauan counterparts, provide more and better medical facilities, and step up fisheries and farming.

War is waged upon the rhinoceros beetle, a huge black creature with a horn like that of a rhino, which killed 99 percent of all coconut trees during World War II. Robert P. Owen, entomologist for the Trust Territory, imported large black wasps from Zanzibar which prey upon the larva of this beetle. The pest is now under control but eternal vigilance is necessary to eliminate possible breeding places. Owen raises thousands of wasps in piles of sawdust back of his laboratory and ships them to any islands bothered by rhinos, including Fiji, Samoa, and the Philippines.

Another ugly intruder is the six-inch African snail. It was brought in during the war by the Japanese when besieged Palau began to feel the pinch of starvation. It did not make a very satisfactory food. It was a disgusting creature, hard to prepare and very tough. Left alone, it multiplied rapidly and swept through vegetable gardens, devouring every green thing. Owen brought in a colony of cannibal snails from Florida. The Florida snails consider their African brothers excellent food. Owen has reason to believe that when the Floridians have destroyed the Africans they will turn upon each other and exterminate themselves. Very neat, if it works.

Belatedly something has been done about Palau's poisonous water supply. For nearly twenty years since a U.S. bomb destroyed the reservoir, drinking water was drawn from cisterns and polluted wells. Two hundred and thirty-nine cases of infectious hepatitis finally compelled the construction of a new water system.

Many other good things have been done. But the undone still far exceeds the done.

As we journeyed about through many-islanded Palau we were confronted by decay at every turn.

Agriculture was in the doldrums. Farmers complained of the lack of incentive. Government help was not what it had been under the farm-minded Japanese who rewarded the farmer with a bonus of six yen for every pig born, ten yen for every acre planted to pineapples, twenty-five yen for planting a hectare of coconuts.

Deep-sea fishing, though there were efforts to revive it, had sunk to the lowest ebb in forty years. The take had been stupendous. In 1937 the catch in Palau was 32,000,000 pounds. Now it was less than one percent of that amount.

"The fish are still here, dying of old age," said Manny Sproat, in charge of agriculture and fisheries for the Trust Territory. Peter Wilson on Palau had big dreams and no way of making them come true. Davis on Truk had told us:

"Last year local trading companies and commissaries in Truk District imported $104,000 worth of canned fish. Imagine! Importing canned fish to a fisherman's paradise!"

The Japanese created scores of small industries—in cultured pearls, mother-of-pearl, tortoiseshell, bêche-de-mer, processing of shark oil for sewing machines, shagreen from sharkskin, lumbering, mining of phosphate and bauxite, construction of pleasant homes and rather distinguished public buildings. Now these activities had either disappeared or sadly dwindled.

There had been innumerable stores selling all imaginable gadgets, cheaply made and cheaply priced. Now, with Japanese goods out of favor, Palauans must buy something expensive or go without.

There had been jobs for all. Any Micronesian could have money if he was willing to work for it. Now there was widespread unemployment, lassitude, juvenile delinquency.

In this "Paris of the South Seas" there had been any number of places of entertainment. Now there was no motion picture theater other than a disreputable tin barn that overcharged for the privilege of viewing pictures thirty years old, no legitimate theater, no opera or musical comedy, no record shop.

There had been bookstores full of eager browsers. Now there was no bookstore.

There had been a flood of magazines and newspapers. Now there was no daily or even weekly newspaper, and magazines, when they came, were many months old.

There had been a good hospital and fully qualified M.D.s. Now there was a better hospital, but not one M.D. in the archipelago. There were some skillful medical practitioners. There was an excellent nurses' training school but as yet no graduate nurse.

The education of Japanese children had rated high priority. There was now no provision for education of American children except a very small "Dependents' School" for the very young, no provision whatever for high school and college age. But education of Palauans had improved.

The Japanese had built street after street of airy, artistic little houses for Japanese personnel. Now there was no American housing better than converted sheet-iron quonsets or the equivalent.

Koror had been a clean and dustless city of paved streets. Now there were no paved streets, no money to maintain unpaved streets, no taxis except ancient jeeps with uncushioned iron seats, few private cars, and no spare parts available.

Some of these conditions will have been improved before this book sees print. But official personnel remains keenly aware that, for lack of means, progress must be slow and painful.

Full allowance must be made for the fact that America started from scratch. Palau had been wrecked by bombs. It was necessary to build from the ground up. But Japan also had to start from scratch when she took over in 1914 from the Germans, who had done little or nothing to develop Palau. Yet in thirty years Japan performed miracles in Palau. We have been in Palau for two-thirds of that time but there is no sign as yet of any miracles.

15

Corals, Caves, and Crocs

FORTUNATELY these shortcomings, however distressing to the Palauan, hardly affect the tourist.

He does not come to the South Pacific to read the papers, see motion pictures, operas and musical comedies, go to school, boil in a quonset. Ensconced in a comfortable hotel, he is free to make expeditions among the two hundred islands of a fascinating lagoon, sail, swim, snorkel, fish, hunt shells and coral on the barrier reef, shoot crocodiles, watch tropical birds, hike down forest trails, climb moderate mountains, and study the evolution, in only half a century, of headhunting savages into the most modernized and progressive citizens of Micronesia. Says Judge Toomin, Associate Justice of the Trust, "If the islands ever join in a national confederation, I predict the Palauans will lead the others."

One outstanding superiority of Palau over more frequented resorts is that the tourist has the place pretty much to himself. In the typical tourist hangout, the tourist sees no one, talks with no one, but fellow tourists. He is insulated from the land and the people by his own kind. It is not so in these islands. He can wander at will without coming on a tour party at every turn. He can enjoy direct contact with the people—not only the natives, but the American residents.

Try that in Hawaii and see how far you get. There, quailing before the tourist flood, the resident makes his home his castle. In Palau there are no castles. Every home is your home. The people, hungry for news of America, receive you with open arms. You are promptly made a member of the community. If you accept all invitations you will never have an evening to yourself. Our social whirl on Majuro, for example, ran thus:

First evening. Cocktail hour and dinner for fifty at the home of the Administrative Officer.

Second. Same at the home of the Distad.

Third. Same at the home of the Assistant Distad.

Fourth. Meeting and dinner of the Mieco Board of Directors.

Fifth. Cocktail party and dinner and improvised vaudeville and dancing at the Coconut Rendezvous Club.

Sixth. Reception and dinner in honor of the new Hicom.

Seventh. Good-bye dinner for us at the home of Ernest and Lindy Milne.

There is no compulsion about it. You may have as much or as little sociability as you wish. Of course such openhanded hospitality will not last. The influx of visitors will, in time, make the open house impracticable.

Palau combines the languorous charm of the atoll with the invigorating freshness of the hills. The trade wind seldom stops to draw breath. Summer is eternal. Though the islands nudge the equator the heat is less than in summertime New York. All the year round the temperature wavers between 70 and 85 degrees Fahrenheit. Thanks to the sun and the sea, the air is warm and cool at one and the same time. Doctors agree that the climate is healthful.

This begins to sound like a travel brochure. It can't be helped; Palau does capture the enthusiasm of the most hardened sightseer. From the mountain ranges one looks down upon a wonderland of pleasant valleys, jade and turquoise lagoon, hundreds of bushy-headed islands, and the white reef edged with robin's-egg blue shallows on one side and blue-black deeps on the other.

The largest island of Palau, and indeed of the entire Trust Territory, is Babeldaob or Babelthuap. There is hardly an island in all Micronesia that is not confusingly spelled in at least two and sometimes half a dozen different ways. On this island there are great uplands covered with grass and groves of fine trees. Pineapple and tapioca grow well, timber is plentiful, and the Japanese planted rubber trees and mined bauxite.

Close to Koror lies an amazing labyrinth of small high islands known as the Rock Islands. Perhaps they might better have been called the Flowerpots. You may sail among them but not climb them, for they rise abruptly from the sea in a limestone cliff leaning outward in the fashion of a flowerpot and culminating at the top in a dense growth of flowering trees and shrubs. On many islands the cliff is so deeply undercut by the waves that a continuous roof runs around the edge of the island and affords from ten to twenty feet of shelter from rain or sun. At places the limestone is still further cut away, making deep caves where crocodiles wait and watch—sea crocodiles, quite savage, twelve to twenty feet in length. I had saved the account of a recent tussle with one of these brutes:

> Masayuki Arurang and Jim Skebong were walking along the shore with flashlights and spears around midnight when they saw the red glare of a crocodile's eyes reflected in their flashlight beams. They threw their spears and one caught the crocodile in the throat. He immediately started to roll, twisting the spear around his neck and causing a great commotion in the shallow water. Arurang and Skebong, seeing that it was an extra large crocodile, called to other men sleeping nearby to come with their spears and help.

Within a short time the crocodile had been speared six more times in the base of the tail so as to weaken it. Two hours of struggle were required before the crocodile tired and it was possible to drag it out on the shore. His mouth was quickly bound up and a large pole tied to his mouth, back and tail to keep him in a semi-straight position and prevent him from whipping about once he recuperated.

The next morning he was loaded on a bamboo raft and towed to the Fisheries Station where he was put on a truck and taken to the entomology zoo to be kept alive for display during the Palau Fair. To help in his recovery from the spear wounds Dr. Masao gave him a healthy dose of penicillin. He was then released in a cage complete with small pool.

After staying in the pool for several days he began to move about and even tried to eat one of his smaller relatives that measured only five feet in length.

Overhead, as we sailed through the maze, white "tropic birds," each with a long pencil of a tail, shared the air with flying foxes, black, ominous, spanning from three to six feet between wingtips. Monitor lizards some seven feet in length make themselves at home in these lofty flowerpots, though how they get there is a mystery.

We landed on a sand beach in Crocodile Cove, an idyllic spot hugged closely by two islands, one of them penetrated by a dark cave running clear through from bay to bay.

We retired into the shrubbery and changed to bathing suits. With Owen I waded into the cave.

"Keep an eye out for crocs," he warned me.

"Have you actually seen any here?"

"Plenty. We killed three—just about where you're standing."

I looked around apprehensively through the half-dark. There was nothing to be seen but some ledges above water along the side of the cave. On these rock shelves were the remains of old fires.

"Strange place to have a picnic," I said.

"It was no picnic. The Japs made those fires. They used all the caves as bomb shelters. Even after the war, a few of them were still hiding here."

It was a relief to get back to the sunny beach. With mask and snorkel we swam out into Crocodile Cove, looking down on a coral pageant, miniature forests, domes and towers, in colors never seen in the land world, swarms of neon-bright small fish, sea urchins with long poisonous black needles, annelid worms with waving flowerlike feelers, and those unique animal chrysanthemums, the sea anemones. We dived for shells—queen's helmet, cowrie, cone, murex, conch, volute. The water was like warm velvet.

We probed other caves. From their roofs hung glistening stalactites, some of great size.

"Money," said Owen.

For a moment I failed to understand him. Then I stumbled against something in the yard-deep water and looked down to see a broken stone disc with a hole in the center. It looked like a millstone. But I recognized it as money, one of the stone coins used as currency on the island of Yap.

Yap is famous for its stone money. It is the only place in the world where stone coinage is used.

How could stone be valuable enough to serve as money?

This stone is stalactite. Yap has no caves and no stalactites. Canoes must come three hundred miles from Yap to Palau, and Yapese stonecutters must spend weeks or months laboriously cutting stalactites into discs, then transport the discs back to Yap. The great weight causes canoes to founder and lives are lost. The labor and risk involved, and the fact that such material is not found on Yap, give the coins their value.

Resuming the journey by launch, we passed the large island of Urukdapel, uninhabited, surrounded by hundreds of small islands, thin-necked and thick-headed, each looking like the bushy head of a giant savage protruding from the sea. Occasionally the launch chugged through a high arch, skeleton of an island otherwise worn away.

This inland sea is quite as beautiful as Japan's own Inland Sea and as picturesque as Matsushima.

We passed the fantastic all-elbows islands of Ailmalk and Aulong, then skimmed over jade green shallows of inexpressible beauty to the island of Peleliu, scene of some of the hardest fighting in the island war. The forest was choked with fallen trees. A few natives had returned and rebuilt their homes. Gorgeous red-and-bronze-green roosters, similar to some in our chicken yards but much more powerful of wing, flew from one lofty treetop to another, screaming as they went.

It was a surprise to meet on this remote island people who spoke our language—not Palauan English but English English. One or the other of their parents or grandparents had been English.

One reason why the Palauans are the most handsome, alert, and progressive of Micronesians is that their blood is not exclusively Malay or Melanesian but to a considerable extent Japanese and English. In fact, the English were among the first foreigners to arrive on these islands.

Civilization, chiefly in the form of rifles and smallpox, came to Palau in a storm on the night of August 9, 1783.

The *Antelope,* schooner of three hundred tons, ran aground on the coral reef. Captain Wilson ordered compass, food, water, arms, and ammunition put into a small boat and took off at

dawn for a small island three miles distant. It was found to be
uninhabited. The ship's goods were gradually transferred from
the wreck to the island, and the crew set about the building of
a new schooner.

But they were not to remain undisturbed. On the twelfth,
eight natives appeared and a Malay who understood English.
They brought a request from the king that the strangers should
visit him upon Koror Island. Matthias, the captain's brother,
courageously offered to be a hostage to fortune and went with
the natives.

He was received cordially by the king, Abba Thulle. After
being regaled on honey tea, coconut meat and taro cakes, he
was given a sleeping mat and a block of wood intended to serve
as a pillow. What with the hardness of the pillow and the wonder of the admiring throng which stood about him all night
(for he was the first white man they had ever seen) he got little
sleep. Moreover a fire was kindled just outside his room . . . he
feared he was to be burned alive, and prayed to God. He did
not know that a fire is always made in honor of a guest. He
returned to camp none the worse and had favorable reports to
make concerning King Abba Thulle.

These auspicious beginnings were promptly spoiled when six
natives under cover of night visited the wreck and stole a
supply of medicines. But retribution followed them swiftly.
Thinking the medicines were food, they drank them down, and
all died. Native respect for the visitors grew. They were
credited with mysterious power.

So the king thought it wise to visit Captain Wilson. He came
naked, but was distinguished by the iron ax he carried on his
shoulder. The common people used axes made of shell.

Captain Wilson ordered his crew to fire a welcoming salute.
The king and his followers, terrified by the explosion, began to
run to their canoes, but finding themselves unharmed, re-

turned full of curiosity about the thunder-sticks. The captain showed them how these strange tubes could be used to break a twig on a distant tree, or kill a bird, although no arrow was seen to pass from the tube to the bird.

A bright idea came to the king. Could not this tube be used to kill men also? The captain complimented him upon the idea, adding that it was not entirely original—others had thought of the same thing.

The king returned the next morning and asked if he could borrow five guns for five days. He was expecting some enemies and wished to surprise them. Wilson lent him the guns and ammunition.

The king's enemies came upon him, one thousand strong in one hundred and fifty canoes. The wild shots of the king's inexperienced marksmen did little damage to the enemy but did happen to pick off one of the king's own men. This so astounded the enemy that they fled. The king's men buried the accidental victim and celebrated a great victory.

Next, the war was carried into the enemy's territory. Some of the Englishmen were persuaded to go along to operate the rifles and the results this time were more positive.

Wars continued, with English help, until the tribes in all directions were under the sway of King Abba Thulle. It does not seem to have disturbed the king that Captain Wilson raised the British flag and fired three times, thus claiming ultimate sovereignty for Great Britain. The king was more powerful than he had ever been before. And on all surrounding islands were the evidences of his prowess—taro fields burned, coconut trees cut down. Civilization was wonderful. The king resolved that his own son should go to England to reap more of the benefits of enlightenment.

The ship was finished. Its hull was printed with red and yellow clay presented by the king. The king asked Wilson to take his second son, Leeboo, to England with him, and Wilson consented.

While the savage prince dreamed of life in England, one of the Englishmen, Blanchard, dreamed with equal ardor of the joys of life on a savage isle. The captain finally consented to leave him behind. Before sailing away, November 12, 1783, Captain Wilson presented the king with five rifles, five shotguns and a barrel of powder. Blanchard, who was an expert rifleman, would teach the king's men the use of these armaments.

The king was overjoyed. He made Blanchard a chief and gave him two women and a forest. Blanchard removed his clothing, tattooed his body, and made every effort to revert to type. Leeboo put on clothes, whitened his skin, and learned English.

After four months in England, Prince Leeboo caught smallpox and died. After seven years in Palau, rifleman Blanchard was killed in battle—by a spear.

In 1790 two English ships, the *Panther* and the *Endeavour,* were sent from Bombay to Palau. Two of the men who had been with the *Antelope* were on board and were recognized by the natives. The king was saddened to hear of the death of his son, but was pleased with the gifts showered upon him: four cows, two oxen, two Bengal sheep, eight goats, five Bombay pigs, three ducks, two geese, one Sumatran wild duck, two hens, one rooster, eight pigeons, two parrots, ammunition, silverware, grindstones, spoons, and saws. In return for these gifts, the king thought it not too much to permit the British formally and officially to raise their flag, declare Palau British territory and build a fortification of stones on Arakabesan. It was called Fort Abercrombie after the governor of Bombay.

Again, one man was enamored of simple savage life. It was Captain McClure of the *Panther.* He turned over the *Panther* to the next in command and stayed on Palau. It is thought that he had ambitions to become the king of Palau. He kept with him twenty rifles, twelve revolvers, twelve axes and a large amount of explosives. His dream of paradise was short-lived, for he came away from the island ill and died an obscure death.

And so, out of this adventure with the English, Palau had gained rifles, livestock, and an assortment of the best civilized diseases. The rifles rusted, the livestock died, but the diseases lived on. The English had gained an empty sovereignty, for there was no way to make use of it. The fort fell to ruins. The British Admiralty forgot Palau. Spain later nonchalantly picked it up and found no trace of the English except a few buff-skinned descendants of Blanchard and McClure and considerable smallpox, tuberculosis, and syphilis.

"No good," we were told by the last king of Koror, a direct descendant of Abba Thulle. "We like to have foreigners come. It is exciting. They show us new things. But sometimes I think it would be better if no foreigners had come—no English, Spanish, Germans, Japanese, Americans, anybody. This is an island. People on an island are supposed to live their own life. It must be so or the gods would not have made it an island. Don't you think so?"

I couldn't answer. It seemed so, indeed. And yet, in a world so crowded and so swiftly traversed, are there any islands any more? Perhaps we are condemned to world brotherhood whether it is good for us or not.

16.

Grass Skirt, Stone Money

HE sat on his heels and stared at us.

"I don't want to go home," he said to our native host. "I want to stay and look at them. I never saw the like!"

"Tell him to stay," I said. "We never saw the like either."

His expression became puzzled. Why should we think *him* strange? Comb a foot long projecting from his bushy hair. Coal-black teeth. Vermilion lips dripping with betel juice. Naked body, liberally tattooed. Scarlet loincloth. He laughed.

"Why, everybody looks like me!"

"Yap" means "The Land." To the Yap native it is the only land, the center of the world.

He rejects with high scorn the tomfooleries of civilization. He believes that to copy alien customs would be to anger the deities of Yap and bring disease and death. Perhaps this is in part a heritage from early times when too close association with malady-bringing foreign sailors did mean just that—disease and death. Therefore the Yap native has, as firmly as his overlords will let him, withdrawn from all contact with the outside world.

Yap is unique. There is nothing else like it in the seven seas.

It is a relic of a forgotten age, the only spot in the Pacific where women are ashamed *not* to show their breasts, the only place on the planet where stone coins up to twelve feet in diameter are used as money.

Four strikingly beautiful islands in a coral lagoon embraced by a coral reef constitute the Yap group. The population was at one time fifty thousand. Contact with the "civilized" world caused it to sink during Spanish, German, and Japanese times to less than three thousand. It is now slowly recovering and at present stands at about six thousand.

The American administration is to be credited with saving the Yapese from extinction. It would have been a sad loss, for these people have qualities hardly to be found elsewhere.

There is no tin shantytown on Yap except one built by the government for public employees. This is on the headquarters island, itself called Yap, and is in the best tradition of the Western slum. The other three islands are Map, Rumung, and Tomil, and here the Yap builder is allowed to have his own way.

On our previous visit we had photographed a small boy up a tree chewing breadfruit gum and plastering it on a branch to catch birds. On this visit we met him again, grown to manhood. We did not recognize him and he had to remind us of our former meeting.

"Come and see my house," he said through our interpreter. "I have just finished it."

We distrustfully walked down the jungle path to our gum-chewer's property. Perhaps he had succumbed to the ambition to go modern. If so, his house would be one room, about twelve feet square, with iron roof, board walls, and stilts raising the structure high enough from the ground to allow for a chicken run and hog wallow beneath.

So what was our delight to be confronted by an artistic creation in the best traditional style, its substantial thatch soaring up steeply to a gable fifty feet above the ground, its walls artfully woven of delicate but durable pandanus leaves, its tall doorposts and broad lintel painstakingly carved to represent legendary Yap heroes.

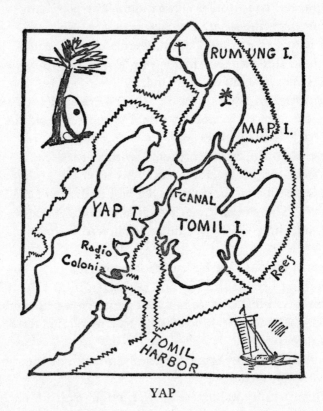

YAP

Within, the house was as cool as if air-conditioned. It was some forty by fifty feet, divided by bamboo screens, and carpeted by reed mats six deep.

We saw many other fine native houses on Map, Rumung, and Tomil, one of the best residences being that of the wealthy Tamaj in the village of Bechiyel. But finer than any private home was the All Men House. Each village had one. It was a clubhouse for male gossip of an evening while the women stayed at home dry-cleaning the dinner dishes with leaves and putting the babies to bed on the bamboo slats. The All Men House is generally perched on a promontory projecting into the lagoon. It is built by a professional architect whose skill has come down to him from father to son for generations.

Map, the loveliest of the Yap group, is the tropic isle of one's dreams. The path winds through a grove of stately coconut trees, heavily loaded—and it is best to dream with eyes uplifted lest the fifty-foot fall of a two-pound nut take one unaware. Nearby is a shadow-patterned sand beach. It slopes gently into a lagoon where a master artist has tried to make a rainbow with green alone, and has succeeded. Dazzled by colors, you begin to count them, and find there is only one. But that one, green, expresses itself in so many tints, shades, hues, and moods that you wonder why nature should ever have considered any other colors necessary. Green is a versatile actor—when supported by the stagecraft of a tropic sun, a battery of kliegs in the form of white breakers on the reef, a black backdrop, a limitless proscenium, and the million footlights of reflecting coral studding the lagoon floor.

On our chart of Map, villages were indicated by large circles such as a map of Europe might use to mark Paris, Berlin, and Rome. But in the coconut forest it is difficult to know when one is in a village. The houses are scattered and well concealed in the woods, apart from the trunk-line path. Very rarely does a village have a Main Street. The Yapese makes full use of the privacy which the jungle affords. The man particularly wants privacy—for his wife. She should be too busy, he thinks, to spend her time in idle chatter with other women. Chatter is man's prerogative; hence the All Men House.

The women also have their clubhouse, but it is not meant for gossip. The *dopal* is the house of childbirth. It is also the prison of the girl who has just reached puberty and is expected to remain in seclusion for some months until she is fully mature. Every woman must spend the few days of menstruation every month in the dopal. It is not, like the All Men House, easy of access. It is often placed on an islet in a reeking swamp so that men may not easily get to it or women escape from it. When anyone has a right to come or go, planks are placed across the waters of the swamp, and later withdrawn, like the drawbridge over a castle moat.

A Yap youth associates intimately with many young girls until he has finally made his choice. A man would not think of marrying a woman without first testing her congeniality by means of premarital relations. Girls are tested before puberty; hence the necessity of the dopal so that they might, for at least a few months while maturing, be undisturbed.

I see in a recent issue of *Holiday* that every All Men House has a *mespil*, a girl who takes up her residence in the clubhouse and is expected to serve the sexual needs of all members. This is correct, except that the tense is wrong. In fairness to the Yapese it should be said that they rejected the mespil custom nearly a half century ago. Changes do take place, even in Yap.

The Yap dwellers have their own peculiar sense of decency. It does not include a ban on nudity. An occasional Yap girl wears a brassiere, but not as intended by the manufacturer. She straps it around her waist and uses it as a pair of pockets to carry betel nuts.

In the jungle village of Weloy we came upon a pretty, barebreasted, grass-skirted young mother nursing her baby. Her teeth were stained with betel juice. Here was a typical island girl the like of which might have been found in the same spot two centuries ago.

Using sign language, we asked if we might take her picture. She replied in perfect English!

Further questioning brought out the fact that she was a member of that most elite intelligentsia of Micronesia, the graduates of the Ponape high school. Upon graduation she had returned quite happily to her beautiful thatch home among the coconut palms, had laid aside her mail-order dress and slipped back easily into the old ways.

But she was full of advanced notions on child care and familiar with the news of the world. Trained in nursing, she was regularly called to serve in the hospital. She was a member of the Business Women's Club—a group of bare-bosomed career girls including nurses, sanitarians, secretaries, typists, and clerks in Yap's only general store.

In the village of Bechiyel we made friends with a braw bare-bosomed lass armed with a savage-looking two-foot knife, and were again surprised when she spoke to us in English.

Her education had not spoiled her for the labors of a jungle housewife. The knife, she said, was for digging taro and we could go with her if we chose. She led the way for a good mile down a jungle trail to the taro patch. There Gilbppin, for that was her name, showed no hesitation or false pride upon wading into the muddy water, lopping off the man-size leaves, then uprooting the thirty-pound tuber. She trimmed and cleaned it as well as anything could be cleaned in water that was half mud. Then she put in two new shoots to take the place of the plant removed.

No more ashamed of her spatters than a soldier of his wounds, she chatted gaily as we carried the tuber back to the village.

It was in the same village that we admired the house of a well-to-do chief who could have built in glass and concrete with patio and swimming pool if he had so desired. But his house was in the best Yap style with its great thatch roof soaring to the tops of the coconut palms.

In the corner lay a bunch of betel nuts, and in the garden grew the *Piper methysticum*. Here was age-old refreshment. I tried it and, unexpectedly, enjoyed it. Crushed betel sprinkled liberally with lime made from burned coral was wrapped in a leaf of *Piper methysticum* and popped into the mouth. It had a hot peppery astringent taste, puckery like unripe persimmon.

Most visitors are inclined to abhor the betel-chewing habit because it reddens the gums and blackens the teeth. Dr. Aaron Jaffe, as Director of the Trust's Dental Services, has found that excessive use of the powdered coral causes inflammation of the necks of the teeth and surrounding soft tissues. On the other hand, he concluded that the black coat over the tooth retards decay. Summing up, betel is far less injurious than carbonated drinks, and leaves no unsightly piles of empty bottles and cans outside the house.

An examination of 278 school children showed only eighteen teeth with caries. This was, in the doctor's words, "astounding in view of the fact that none of these children had previously received dental treatment and many had never used a toothbrush. The low caries rate is directly attributable to their diet which is predominantly taro and fish. The latter food provides them with calcium, phosphorus, and oil substances needed for the building of good sound teeth."

Mary commented on the beautiful grass skirt worn by the chief's wife who said, "You like? I give you one."

She brought out a fresh skirt, newly made. "Try it on."

Mary tried it on and remarked about its weight.

"Especially when it is green and the leaves are still full of

The administrator of Yap objected to bare breasts. He prescribed T-shirts. But then the women couldn't nurse their babies, so they cut two round holes in the T-shirt. "I give up," said the official.

Bejeweled, perfumed, painted, a girl is prepared to take
part in a traditional dance.

The dance costume may be barbaric but the camera is modern. The wooden comb is allowed only to a member of a noble family.

Twins are "bad luck." So by order of the village elders one is being sold to another village. Payment will be three pieces of stone money. The mother is not too happy about it.

The broad mouth allows room for healthy teeth, found by dentists to be remarkably free of caries because of the simple island diet.

The Micronesian is a happy blend of Polynesian, Melanesian, Mongol and Japanese with a dash of sea-captain English.

The extended ear lobe is useful for carrying packages. But it is in the way when there is work to be done and is then knotted neatly about the ear.

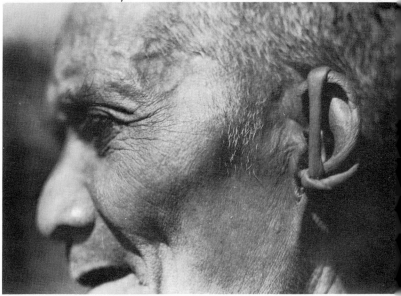

Heavy-footed mermaid. The grass skirt, even when not soaked with sea water as this is, may weigh thirty pounds.

The sail of the outrigger is made of interlaced leaves of pandanus.

Gum, wound on a stick, snares birds attracted by the ripe papaya.

No water bill to pay. Rain water trickles down the tree
to be captured in a handmade jar.

The telephone, island version. The old chief blows on the shell known to science as the Tritonium and to mythology as Triton's Horn, to call the men to the council house.

When the Japanese left they took their modern tools with them, and the island carpenter reverted to the use of the prehistoric drill.

American administrators are making heroic efforts to equal their predecessors, the Japanese, in the agricultural training of young islanders.

moisture," agreed the woman. "But it is heaviest after you go in swimming. When you come out it weighs about thirty pounds."

"But why wear this in the water? Don't you use a bathing suit?"

The woman looked shocked. "That is not our custom. It may be all right for you but not for us. We consider the bathing suit immodest. How can a woman wear something that shows so plainly the shape of her body below the waist!"

So it became clear that Yap propriety is one thing above the belt line and quite another below.

It takes only a few days to become used to this difference in values. In Yap a brown male body looks quite right in nothing but a breechclout; and a fragrant, freshly made grass skirt with its swing and its rustle can be charming. There is a little more cover-up in the port town, but even there, G-strung gentlemen wander through the store between cans of American-made soup and jars of chewing gum, and girls bare-breasted and bare-footed attend divine service. The mother hubbard has never conquered Yap.

Captain Roberts of the schooner *Roque* which sails through the islands collecting copra told us of a former Distad in Yap who resolved that Yap women must cover their bosoms. But with what? T-shirts were adopted. They were bought and distributed, and the women put them on.

But then they could not nurse their babies. So they snipped two large holes in the T-shirt. Of course the brown fountain-heads protruding from the white shirt were more conspicuous than they had been in their natural surroundings. The Distad threw up his hands.

"I give in!"

A district director of education, Vincent Edson, approved the *thu* or G-string and the grass skirt as proper school costumes. In too many cases pupils wearing Western clothes did not keep either themselves or their clothing clean. But a bare body is easily cleaned, and a grass skirt is readily replaced at no expense.

The Yapese are not averse to change—but they insist that the change be sensible.

$$\mathfrak{V}$$

It was on a trail through the woods of Tomil. A man coming the other way stopped short and gazed at us as if we were ghosts. Then he broke into a smile.

"I thought you were dead," was his disconcerting greeting. "Do you remember me? My name is Matam. Come to my house. I have something to show you."

We walked with him a short distance up a side path and entered his basketlike home.

He fished about in a pile of papers, drew out a copy of *National Geographic* for June 1942 and opened it at page 776 to a picture of a stone coin twelve feet in diameter. Matam himself had shown us the stone during our earlier visit. The coin had been standing on edge and Mary, to demonstrate its size, had coiled up like a watch spring in the hole. A priest, Matam said, had given him the magazine, and he had kept it ever since.

"The money," I said, "is it still here?"

"Just where it was," he replied. "But it has fallen down. Come, I will take you."

Only two minutes' walk, and he stopped. "There it is."

We could see nothing but a pile of brush. But there was a slight glint of stone through the leaves. We cleared away the twigs and creepers and there was the great coin.

Matam looked at Mary and at the hole and grinned. "Do it again," he suggested.

Mary tried. She was not quite as good a watch spring as she

had been nearly thirty years before when the picture was taken.

She stood up and looked at the hole. "I'm sure it was bigger than that. Could it have shrunk?"

"Does it belong to the same people who owned it when we were here?" I asked Matam.

"Oh no. It has changed owners many times. Now it belongs to a village on the other side of the island."

Stone money, for which Yap is famous, is still valued and still used. The coins vary in diameter from six inches to a dozen feet. A large coin weighs several tons. Each coin has a hole in the center through which a pole may be thrust for carrying purposes.

This works very well for coins of moderate size, but the enormous ones remain *in situ.* Title to such a coin may pass from one owner to another, but everyone knows the owner and there is no need to move it. A small coin only a foot or so in diameter will be kept in the owner's house. Coins too large for the house will be lined up like a fence around his property. A great coin is not owned by an individual but by a village. It is used for big transactions only. If the village wishes to buy a large boat, or engage the services of a village famous for its skill in building an All Men House, the great coin may pay the bill—but it stays where it is.

The Yapese sometimes sell one of their coins, but reluctantly. A coin five feet in diameter was bought by the Money Museum of the National Bank of Detroit for $125 (a going rate of $25 a foot). After the coin had been shipped the seller had remorseful afterthoughts and tried to get it back.

There is a dollar economy also in Yap, but that does not lessen the value of the ancient coins. Yapese oldsters say:

"When we were young Spanish money was good. Then the Germans came and Spanish money was no good. Then the Japanese came and German money was no good. Then the Americans came and Japanese money was no good. Stone money is always good."

At the south end of the main island we saw a gang of men building a motor launch.

"How will they be paid?" I asked.

The boss pointed to a row of stone coins each about three feet in diameter standing on edge, a bamboo carrying pole thrust through the hole of every coin.

Here was striking evidence that the ancient currency is still in actual use.

In a village on Tomil we sympathized with a young mother, one of whose twin babies was about to be taken from her for adoption in another village.

The reason for this action was obscure. In many parts of the world primitive tribes consider twins unlucky, and one must be killed or otherwise disposed of. Here there was no thought of killing the surplus twin, but it was to be taken away, and the mother was not happy about it.

Outside the house under the trees a circle of men, some from this village, some from the adopting village, discussed terms. It would be too crude to say that the child was to be paid for, but a ceremonial gift must be made by the adopting village to the village of the child's parents. The visitors had brought their proposed gift, a three-foot stone coin, and after much palaver it was accepted.

The child must have been much desired to warrant the gift of a coin worth $75 if sold abroad. Stone money is still highly regarded and, according to our native-born anthropologist friend, even pieces lying half covered with moss and leaf mold and apparently abandoned are well known and valued.

How did Yap get such an unwieldy coinage? The tradition is

that a thousand years ago one of the more disreputable gods thought to cause dissension among men. They were at peace because they had nothing to war over. He would give them something to war over. Money.

He whispered to a king of Tomil a plan to make him great and powerful. Obedient to the heavenly vision, the king sailed south over unknown waters to islands of the Palau group. There he found shining rock (stalactite) which the malicious deity instructed him to have his men hew out with their shell axes into flat pieces rounded like the orb of the full moon. These were loaded into the canoe and brought to Yap, not without many perils. The god cast a spell over the people that caused every man of them to desire nothing so much as one of these heaven-sent stones. To obtain them, they paid the king of Tomil great riches in the form of coconuts, canoes and houses. So the wheels became a medium of exchange for goods.

And those who tell the legend go on to say that there has been no peace in Yap since then. The golden (or stone) apple of discord disrupted the island paradise. Formerly there had been no covetousness, for there was nothing to covet. No man desired his neighbor's coconuts, for he had his own. There was food enough for everyone and no one wanted clothing. Greed was born when money came in. There was quarreling among relatives as to who should inherit which rock. Feuds between neighbors. Wars between villages. The elders of Yap, ignorant of the fact that the Bible agrees with them, have their own bitter reasons to believe that the love of money is the root of all evil.

"Nine quarrels out of ten are over money," one told me.

How the god must have laughed!

There was only enough of the first money to be tantalizing. Expeditions set out to get more. Many canoes were lost, partic-

ularly on the return voyage when loaded to the danger point
with great stone wheels. It was not uncommon for twenty canoes to set out and only one return.

Of course the difficulty and danger in securing the stone kept
up its value. There could be no counterfeiting, for there was no
similar stone to be found in Yap.

These goings-on amused not only the god but an Irishman
named O'Keefe.

Buccaneer O'Keefe cast anchor in Yap harbor during the
Spanish rule (a rule that was largely characterized by the lack
of any) and proceeded to look the natives over with a view to
making what he could out of them. He soon found that they
would give copra, fish, women, anything they possessed, for
stone money.

Very well, stone money they should have. He had heard that
large pieces were especially in demand. That was where he
fitted in. On his schooner he could transport pieces many times
as large as could be carried in canoes.

I found on the island of Palau a cross-eyed old native sailor
with the shamrock tattooed on his brown skin who had sailed
with Captain O'Keefe for years. He told me the story.

"He came to Palau and went to the king. He asked for many
men to help dig stone money.

"The king said, 'What will you give?'

"The captain gave rope. He gave paint to paint the bodies of
the dead. Dye to color lava-lavas. And some guns. He promised
to give more when the work was done.

"The men of Palau dug . . . many months, years. Small
stones took little time. But it took two years to dig out a great
wheel.

"He kept taking the wheels to Yap and selling them to the
natives for copra.

"But the chiefs of Palau became angry because he paid no

more and was cruel to the men. They looked for a chance to punish him."

The opportunity came when Captain O'Keefe was wrecked in the Palau group at Alklung. The natives seized all his goods. But this punishment was not enough.

"Now we'll give you what you gave us." They lashed him to a tree and brought out a cat-o'-nine-tails salvaged from his own ship. They flogged him.

After his release he lost no time in lodging complaint at Hong Kong. A warship visited Palau and demanded an indemnity in the form of large quantities of copra and bêche-de-mer from the offending village of Alklung.

Time passed and the indemnity was not paid. Then came two warships, the H.M.S. *Lily* under Captain Evans and the H.M.S. *Comus* under Captain East. Their men landed and burned the village to the ground. The people fled to the interior. Captain Evans was in favor of pursuing and exterminating them. But Captain East, old and kindly, said, "They have run away. Let be."

Upon return to England, Captain Evans complained, "It was impossible to do anything on Palau, because of East."

So Captain East was considered too old and gentle to teach the savages of the South Seas due respect for the white man. He lost his command.

Captain O'Keefe sowed trouble by supplying the natives with guns—but he was not the only trader to do that. For one gun he demanded fifty five-gallon cans of turtle shell, or fifty rice bags of bêche-de-mer.

He married a native woman of Nauru. And since her younger sister didn't want to be left alone, he married her too. The two wives seemed to find it an ideal arrangement. They lived together happily on a charming islet of Yap, their joint spouse being most of the time away on one foray or another.

Several old chiefs of Yap and Palau recalled only too well how the doughty captain had taken a gang of natives to work on his island Mapia, near New Guinea . . . and left them there. He said it was too much bother to bring them back. The survivors finally attracted the attention of a passing ship and were rescued.

"When he saw a girl he liked," said a reminiscing chief, "he would take. A pig—'Put it on board, I'll eat it.' No pay. Bad man. But when the Germans came they stopped his wild tricks."

Life lost its savor after that for the burly and jovial buccaneer. The Germans hedged him in with *verbotens*. One day he stocked his schooner for a long voyage, kissed his wives and a few other ladies good-bye, and sailed away. He never came back. Some say that he went to an island known only to him, for he was an excellent navigator and knew the South Seas as few men did. Others suppose that he was lost at sea.

However that may be, he left behind him monuments that will stand to his memory for thousands of years. The largest coin of his minting lies at the bottom of Yap harbor. While being transferred from the schooner's deck to a raft, it slid into the water. The old men who saw it swear that it was twenty feet wide . . . but that may be a fish-that-was-lost measurement.

The great museums naturally want some of these monoliths, unique in the history of the world's coinage. They have taken a few of the smaller ones; but have not yet undertaken to bargain with the natives for a giant stone, remove it without benefit of motor truck, and ship it to the other side of the world.

The people of Yap are as original as their money. Surely it is original to want nothing from anyone. The Yapese do not wait for government favors. When convinced that a thing should be done, they do it themselves. They put up school buildings and dispensaries and finance them out of their own pockets—or breechclouts.

Their spirit of independence was well demonstrated when a UN mission interviewing a council of chiefs said, "Now tell us what we can do for you. What do you need?"

On some other islands this question had brought a torrent of requests. But the Yapese chiefs looked at each other in silence. Then their spokesman rose and said courteously, "If we need anything, we will let you know."

A Yap beggar could not be imagined. Social security would be laughed to scorn. Anyone in need is taken care of by his relatives or friends.

I don't want to give the idea that this is the isle of the blest. It has its shadows. One is faith, now slowly dying, in the powers of the medicine man.

As we followed a path through a dark and eerie woodland our companion, Micronesian anthropologist Francis Defngin, broke silence with:

"You wanted to see a *machamach*. There's one coming."

The machamach or magician was a little wrinkled old man, naked except for a red *thu* about his loins. Seeing us, he seemed about to plunge into the underbrush. We stopped and Defngin went forward alone to speak to him.

"Ask him if we can see his place," I suggested.

I didn't expect Defngin to succeed in this project, for we had found on our previous visit that access to a machamach's house of magic is almost impossible. But I underrated the persuasive power of our friend. It took plenty of talk, as everything does in these islands, but at last the wizard's head moved affirmatively and Defngin signaled us to come on.

The machamach, Yonolang by name, led us uphill by an almost imperceptible path. Finally he stopped and spoke to Defngin.

"He says your wife should stay here. Women may not go further."

Mary sat down on a rock and we plunged into a pathless tangle of brush and thorns, fallen logs, and creeping vines, turning this way and that to avoid obstructions until I completely lost all sense of direction. After a long battle with the brush, Defngin suddenly stopped and said, "Here we are." I could see nothing but more brush shutting us in closely on all sides.

Then in the gloom I made out a piece of sheet iron a few yards square, one edge of it resting on the ground and the other propped to a height of about three feet. Around it lay a number of conch shells. The place was almost smothered in foliage. The machamach crawled under the iron roof, turned about and sat, crossing his legs, and gazed at us with all the calm and dignity of a Buddha.

Dangling from the roof were herbs, bones, skins of lizards, hair of bat, charms made of pieces of coral, and, most important, the *rut* or magic wand made from the poisonous barb of the stingray.

Through Defngin, I asked about the conchs.

"He says he blows on the conch to ensure good weather. He is paid for this service by people who wish to hold a feast, ceremony or dance and want to be sure it won't rain."

"Does he have magic to heal the sick?"

The answer was more modest than I expected. "No, but he can prevent sickness."

"Can he put a curse on someone?"

A generation ago the answer would have been an unqualified yes, but the remaining magic workers now stand in fear of the authorities. The machamach was a bit cagey on this subject and would say only that if a rival magician tried to foil his magic he could kill him.

"Are you teaching a disciple who will carry on your art after you die?"

The question seemed to sadden the old man. "My disciple became a Christian. He believes in the new medicine and will not learn my ways. So I have no heir."

His heirs, whom he would not be willing to acknowledge, are the doctors, nurses, sanitarians, who, though aware that there is something of value in island medical lore, are trying to supplement it with the discoveries and advances of a new age.

17.

Cinderella

OF all the Forgotten Sisters, Yap is the most severely neglected.

The Japanese are partly to blame. They got us off to a bad start on Yap. The devastation caused by Allied bombers was exceeded by the devastation carried out by the Japanese defenders. Besieged Japanese troops, made cruel by desperation, destroyed hundreds of native houses because they needed the wood and thatch as fuel to boil the salt out of seawater. They smashed the foundation platforms to make piers. They broke up the precious stone money to build roads. A survey in 1929 had counted 13,280 pieces of stone money on Yap. After the war there were about six thousand.

Village life was completely disrupted. The men were packed off to the main island to work on the airfields. Or they were put to work in the nickel and copper mines near Gatchepar—without pay.

Overbearing soldiers felt free to confiscate the second most precious possession of the Yapese after stone money. This precious thing was the Yap pig. It is not only the most prized food, but it is the most cherished pet. A small pig is carried in the arms as lovingly as if it were a kitten and it is not uncommon to see a baby nursed at one breast and an infant pig at the other.

Troops put up signs on taro patches, THIS TARO BELONGS TO TROOP —. If the owner of the patch tried to take some of his own taro, he was slapped down.

The soldiers enjoyed liberties that had never been allowed to Japanese civilians. Yapese wives were raped; children who got in the way were disposed of; sick or disabled men were flogged.

We walked through the forest village of Gatchepar with anthropologist Defngin, Seling who had previously been the king of this area, and ethnologist Dr. Inez de Beauclair. The once busy village was now almost deserted. On every side lay the ragged ruins of homes, broken fragments of stone money.

King Seling had owned two large houses. He showed us where they had been. When he and his friend Defngin protested, the officer who heard the complaint assigned them both to payless common labor with pick and shovel in the airfield.

The king showed us his present home—a hut made of half-burned boards and scraps of tin.

Dr. Beauclair, doing what she could to rehabilitate the unfortunate villagers, took us to her own quarters. Here was not the comfortable, spacious home of an official or a missionary. Her "house" was an eight-by-ten thatch room on stilts. There was no running water, no electricity, no refrigerator, no air conditioning, no telephone, no bathroom except the lagoon which at high tide came up among the stilts. She had only to descend a few steps to take a swim.

The villagers brought her fruit, scarce because of a recent typhoon. She admitted that she got hungry for meat and bread. The place was completely divorced from white civilization except by boat, and she had no boat.

"But it costs me almost nothing to live," she said cheerfully.

One thing she had—the absolute adoration of the people she

served. She was not a member of the Peace Corps—yet this was
the Peace Corps idea carried to the nth degree. Actually she
had not been expected to do anything for the villagers, but
merely to study them, having received this assignment from the
Institute of Ethnology of the Academia Sinica in Formosa.

Just as devoted, but more pleasantly housed, was the Distad
of Yap District, Roy Gallemore. If there was anything he or his
wife did not do for the public welfare, it was because the Yapese would not have it or Congress would not pay for it.

With him we bounced south over the most frightful roads we
had found anywhere. There were two seats in the jeep, the one
behind the wheel occupied by the Distad, the other a foot wide
shared by the two passengers. At any moment one or the other
of us left the seat as if shot from a gun. Where there was not a
rock there was a hole. And always there was a rut a foot or more
deep. A steering wheel was really unnecessary; the ruts alone
could have held the car on its course.

The jeep was an exhausted survivor of Navy days. It rattled
like a maraca. "In the repair shop half the time," said Gallemore. But the Distad was lucky. Being the Distad, he had the
best of the fleet.

On Sunday fourteen members of the American colony
dressed in their Sunday best and went to church—by truck.
The seat was occupied by the driver and two ladies. The remaining eleven churchgoers stood in the back of the truck,
clutching each other to avoid being tossed overboard, branches
whipping their faces, a following wind enveloping them in
dust. The vehicle drew up at the church steps with an expiring
gasp. Something had been jolted loose. Noisy repairs went on
during the service, but proved vain. We walked back.

The really serious effects of bad roads and poor transport are felt by the Yapese themselves. They can move only on foot or by boat. Either way, it takes too long to get to market. In the tropical heat, products of farm and garden spoil before they reach town. Children far from school go untaught. Many sick die before they can be brought to the hospital. Villages are isolated, jungle-bound, culturally starved.

There had been 118 miles of good gravel road on Yap during the Japanese regime. Now there were less than thirty. The rest of the highway system had gone back to jungle. All things considered, the statement in the official *Handbook of Information* was modest:

> Vehicle traffic to some parts of the island is impossible and to others, difficult.

The Germans had dug a canal to provide a short cut from Yap to Map. The Japanese preserved the canal and spanned it with two good stone bridges—which became war casualties. In twenty years Public Works has not been able to clear the canal properly or rebuild the bridges.

Still more deplorable is transportation to the outer islands, beautiful lagoon-type atolls scattered over the sea to the east for seven hundred miles. The *Handbook* informs us, with what sounds almost like pride, that these islands are "usually reached on field trips about once every two to three months."

The undone jobs of Yap are so numerous as to distress any UN visiting mission, no matter how friendly.

Recently official visitors found Yap landowners still excluded from their own property because shells two decades old but still alive lay in the soil. Hand grenades, mortars, live artillery ammunition, had not yet been cleared away and the remains of fighter planes cluttered the ground.

A nine-member White House survey mission visiting Yap in 1963 found native employees of the government living in a slum of jerry-built shacks close to the administrative center. No American employee would tolerate such housing.

The presidential survey commission had another shock when they visited the hospital. In the maternity ward a mother lay on bloody sheets that had not been changed since the birth of her child twenty-four hours before. The operating room was open to flies. Spiders spun cobwebs in the corners. A sterilizer and a stethoscope were exposed to dust filtering into the room from the unpaved street. The same dust had brought on an infection in the eyes of the commission's chairman and he requested treatment. He was handed a tube of salve.

"But this medicine went out of date years ago," he said. "It's marked for use before September, 1958."

The protest surprised the medical practitioner. "Most of our medicine is like that," he said.

If there is a world outside of Yap, the Yapese are scarcely aware of it. They do have a newspaper, if one may give a mimeographed sheet so dignified a name. It is called *Tamilang* (Light). It is a very weak ray in the darkness. It is not a daily, nor a weekly, nor a monthly. It is published "now and then"— mostly then. During our visit it was suspended because the typist-mimeographer had quit to have a baby.

There was no broadcasting station on Yap. Shortwave could bring in Manila or Hong Kong or Tokyo—but who could afford shortwave?

I climbed the hill back of the town to the small home of Father F. C. Bailey, head of the mission that has served Yap for three hundred years. He, like Dr. Beauclair, is content with a Peace-Corpslike standard of life and service. He was critical of official policy which, he thought, put Americans first.

"The money goes mainly for the salaries of Americans and

maintenance of facilities for them. For instance, right now there is a furor about the power shortage. This doesn't mean a thing to the people on Map. They have no electricity anyhow. It's purely an American concern. There are too many Americans here and they think too much of their own comfort. And they come and go, like leaves before the wind. The British would have a District Officer in a place like this and that's about all—and he would *stay*."

Perhaps this was an extreme view, born of the father's own unusual sense of dedication. Visiting missions do not find the American staff rolling in luxury and idleness, nor lacking in faithfulness, though their efforts may sometimes be misdirected.

The chief failure to date is the failure to restore agriculture. Nothing means more to the islander than the ability to produce wealth from the soil.

We found the agricultural station only a pale ghost of what it had been in Japanese times. The station was not even reopened until 1954, nine years after the war's end. It consists of six acres of land and a few small buildings.

The new agriculturist—he had been on the job only a few months—had little to show us. "I'm just getting squared away," he said.

He had planted three thousand cacao seedlings for later distribution to farmers. He intended to experiment in trees—citrus, mangosteen, mango, avocado, and others. He visualized reforestation of bare hills of the southern uplands with various pines of the South Pacific.

He had six extension agents in the various islands. These were paid by the government, but there were also sixteen municipal agents paid, not by the government, but by the Yap Congress. This self-help was unique in the Trust Territory.

He took us on a tour of the chicken coops, inhabited by several hundred New Hampshire Reds. He was selling two hundred chicks a month at twenty-five cents each. The Yapese raise fowl for the meat only. They have not been educated to care for the eggs.

Education is really the principal job of the agricultural department. The director must be a good teacher. He must battle with the caste problem. High-caste Yapese will not buy meat or vegetables produced by persons of low caste.

The great economic hope of Yap is the coconut. Yap is the coconut Eden of the Pacific. A congenial soil and thirty years of Japanese coaxing produced a nut so superior that orders for unsprouted nuts poured in from islands all the way from New Guinea to Tahiti.

War bombs destroyed coconut plantations and neglect has deteriorated the quality of the nuts. Recovery has been slow. It has been difficult to find a non-Japanese agriculturalist with the Japanese green thumb.

Nothing is more important to the Yapese than the coconut. What the date palm means to the Sahara oasis, the coconut palm means to the Pacific atoll. Without the versatile and ubiquitous coconut, human life would have been impossible on many islands. You can eat the meat, drink the water from the nut, drink the milk from the flowering stem, prepare syrup or candy from the kernel, get drunk on toddy made from the fermented juice.

One tree may carry ten or fifteen bunches of nuts, each bunch containing from ten to twenty nuts. So every tree is a vertical farm of no mean proportions. It will grow in sand. It does not, like most farms, produce only once or twice a year. It produces continuously. Any day of the year one may take from it a ripe nut ready for copra, a green nut for drinking and eating, and flower stalks that have not yet materialized into nuts. Nor does it get tired like many farms and require a year's rest. It never needs to lie fallow. Typhoons do it little harm. A month before our visit to Yap a typhoon had demolished everything that put up a resistance. The elastic palm trunk, bending before the gale, had conquered by yielding.

The ordinary farm produces only food. But this sky farm poised on its pedestal fifty to ninety feet above the ground will send down almost anything man needs.

Its mighty eighteen-foot leaves made up of leaflets three feet long will provide roof and walls for his house and mats for his floor. Also a lava-lava for him and a skirt for his wife. And hats which, if he does not deign to wear, he may carry to town for sale to sun-fearing foreigners. And a basket to carry them in. And a fan to temper the heat of the trip. And a walking stick; or a bundle of them to sell to strangers who prize them for their lightness and strength. The midrib of the leaflets supplies thread. The fiber of the husk makes good rope. (The husk is soaked in water until the fibers separate. They are then dried and woven.) This rope ties together the beams and pillars of his house, which are probably built of coconut trunks. His fishing nets are made of this fiber. It can also be used to weave a soft fabric, more diaphanous and durable than silk. A slice of the fibrous husk is his torch, unless he has a lamp, in which case the nut supplies the oil.

The same oil generously applied to his body safeguards him from colds and pneumonia in case of long exposure to seawater. In certain islands where clothing has become *de rigueur* and oil is no longer applied because it stains clothing, pulmonary troubles are a matter of grave concern.

His canoe, if not hollowed from a single tree, can be pieced together with boards of coconut. Fallen trunks can be reduced to charcoal as fuel. The leaves and dried shells also make excellent fuel.

Empty shells are his dishes. He can, but seldom does, make soap from the oil. Various medicines and medicants are obtained from the roots. Whenever the islander needs anything, his mind seems to turn first to the coconut palm.

Taboos and superstitions handicap the native farmer. It is said that the gods will laugh at the man who farms. Farming is woman's work. Men should fight. Or, if there is no fighting to do, they should sit in the cool shade of the All Men House and talk endlessly about fighting. They may even get into a fight among themselves over the question of fighting someone else. They vary the monotony by going fishing.

Farming—they do not give it a thought. But it is necessary to give farming a thought, and many a thought, if it is to be successful. Even Yap women regard farming as something unworthy and to be got through with as thoughtlessly as possible.

Moreover, legend says that the gods showed mankind how to farm at the beginning of creation. If any different methods are adopted, the gods will be insulted.

Agriculture is a matter of magic, the Yapese believe, not of natural law. You employ the machamach to wave in the air his wand made of the barbs of the stingray and put a blessing on your taro patch and a curse on your enemy's. You wrap a fruit tree in a magic palm leaf to protect it from birds or thieves. (Incidentally, the same leaf can be put around your wife to make her taboo to other men.) In many parts of the world there is magic to bring rain. But in these tropic isles where rain is too plentiful, there are ceremonies to *stop* rain. It is taboo to take a blue starfish out of the sea. That will surely bring rain, for it is symbolic of the disappearance of the blue sky overhead.

The Japanese overcame many of these taboos by brute force. A slap, a kick, or a punch in the solar plexus was effective when argument failed. The policeman's club was the great educator.

The new regime must get along without these sadistic expedients. So the process is inevitably slower, and is further slowed by lack of experience, aptitude, and money.

18.

Want a Job in Paradise?

WANTED: By U.S. Government, men and women for interesting, well-paid jobs on tropical island, beautiful scenery, equable year-round climate, five-day week, swimming, boating, fishing, Civil Service rating and pay plus 25 percent bonus, low living expenses, tax-free imports, two-year contract renewable. Apply Trust Territory of the Pacific Islands.

So Robert Trumbull, *New York Times* foreign correspondent, suggests that the Trust might advertise the attractions of service in the far Pacific.

But the Trust does not advertise. Instead of seeking publicity, America's blushing colony is inclined to avoid it. This is not only because colonies are now in disfavor, but because the islands are a nest of present or potential military bases and therefore entitled to a certain amount of privacy.

By White House order, this policy of secrecy, involving the exclusion of visitors, has now been officially discarded.

But the habits of two decades resist change. Visitors are now admitted, even welcomed, but no great effort is made to attract them. It is harder to get news out of Micronesia than to get blood from a turnip. Most news-media editors scarcely know it exists. The dislocated worker who would give his eye teeth for a job on a tropical island thinks of the Peace Corps and the Foreign Service but is quite unaware of opportunities in the Trust Territory.

Yet the Trust needs him, needs him desperately, particularly if he has any specialized skill. Even if he has only natural ability a position may be open to him where he can learn as he goes.

There is a continuing demand for teachers. Reports the Education Department: "More than 180 elementary, secondary, administrative and supervisory positions must be filled to meet the requirements of the accelerated education program."

There are open doors in the departments of agriculture, communications, public health, finance, property and supply, public works. There are chairs waiting for secretaries, typists, clerks, accountants, lawyers, electricians, engineers, carpenters, mechanics, and executives who know something about commercial fishing.

There is a personnel director, but his chief task appears to be not to paint the charms of the island paradise, but to warn applicants of the drawbacks and difficulties. It is better to be discouraged at the start than to be disappointed after a two-year contract has been signed. So Personnel stresses the isolation, the heat, humidity, rainfall, cultural differences, psychological problems. Anyone who comes out of this cold bath still glowing with enthusiasm is promising material.

Misfits are the plague of the Administration. There are too many of them—too many square pegs in round holes. Former High Commissioner Nucker was asked by President Eisenhower to describe the chief problem of the territory. He answered, "Americans."

This is not because Americans are Americans, but because

America has had little experience in operating colonies. As James Ramsey Ullman points out:

> The United States has no equivalent of the British Colonial Service, which recruits and trains young men for governmental work in the earth's far corners; and few of the Trust Territory positions are even under our Civil Service, with its concomitant benefits and security. . . . There is, on the one hand, neither the machinery for preparing a man for a career in the islands, nor, on the other, the rewards to make it attractive once he has undertaken it. So career men are what the T.T. rarely gets. What it *does* get is a miscellany of scientists, scholars, idealists, and—let's face it—plain South Seas escapists. And while they unquestionably make for a more stimulating group than a parcel of professional bureaucrats, it's doubtful if they're the world's best at conducting routine government business.*

It is well to be warned before one makes the eight- or ten-thousand-mile journey to the most distant and least-known region on earth under the Stars and Stripes. Anyone who expects life in the South Seas to be an uninterrupted idyl is soon disillusioned.

There *is* heat. After all, the islands are within ten degrees of the equator. It is not comparable to the summertime heat of New York or Los Angeles, but it ranges between 75 and 85 degrees and it is accompanied by humidity of about 80 percent which provokes mildew on clothing and mold on shoes unless they are kept in a hot locker.

With these qualifications, the climate is close to ideal, and remains so the year round.

The refreshing trade wind blows night and day. Usually its caress is as soft as the brush of a dove's wing. But not always. Judge Toomin on his first small-boat trip from Arno to Majuro was so distressed by the wild heaving and keeling and lurching

Where the Bong Tree Grows (World Publishing Company).

through drenching seas that he leaned over and said plaintively to the native skipper, "Is it always like this?"

"Oh no," he answered. "Sometimes it's rough."

And sometimes, often in fact, the surface of the lagoon is like glass. Then, if the moon is shining, and the village lights are reflected in the still water, and the boatmen are singing, the word "paradise" roots itself more firmly than ever in your imagination.

Your island home may not be a dream house. Most members of the staff are embalmed in iron coffins, the quonsets left over from Navy days. These were originally intended to serve for about three years but have now almost reached the decrepit old age of twenty. Some new houses of concrete block are being erected but you must rank high to get one. Even the high and mighty must put up with many inconveniences.

On "Nob Hill" where the chief officials of Truk reside, two new arrivals, Associate Chief Justice Philip Toomin and his wife, were dismayed to find their home a rusty quonset on a viewless lot covered with tangled grass and scraggly weeds. The furniture was rickety, the tables ring-marked, the stove encrusted, the beds looked as if they had been rained on, and the screens were perforated by holes big enough to admit bats and birds.

But an undaunted housewife can work wonders. Pauline Toomin plugged up the openings, put boards under sagging mattresses, planed down chest drawers so they would go in and out, redecorated with paint and wallpaper that she had brought with her from Illinois, and emerged victorious with one of the most attractive places on the island.

She hired a yard boy who spoke only one English word, *Yes,* and a maid somewhat better equipped. They cost one dollar a day each.

Flowers and vegetables were planted and grew well until a

heavy rain brought out the six-inch African snails which promptly devoured everything green. The newcomers learned to grow pest-resistant indigenous plants: bougainvillea, lantana, mango, papaya, pineapple, banana, and coconut.

The judge had his own problems. In his black robe, he suffered under the iron roof of the quonset courtroom. The judge's bench was a seat of torture; "too uncomfortable" complained Judge Toomin, "for even a few minutes' slumber during a dull trial." There were too few seats—most of the spectators sat on the concrete floor. The floor was comparatively cool, particularly when wet. The floor level was below the outside ground level, therefore every brisk rain inundated the courtroom.

The law library was scantily supplied with out-of-date law books. The two Chief Justices had each his own not-so-private office separated by only a five-foot partition, enabling the two to converse without leaving their chairs.

The principal difficulty, however, was not physical, but mental and legal. American notions of justice had to be modified out of respect for the local customs of the island from which the litigants hailed. And since no two islands had quite the same customs, detailed knowledge of the intricacies of native tradition was necessary and justice had to be administered not merely with firmness but with sympathy and understanding.

The exiled Americans, even if forewarned, can have little idea of what they are getting into when they cast in their lot with a handful of American executives, office workers, teachers, doctors, and construction engineers marooned on a desert island.

"It takes some dedication," admitted Florence Shook, secretary to the Chief Justice.

But she went on to point out the advantages. She loved her work; her passage from the homeland and back was paid by the Trust; her salary was good and was supplemented by a 25 percent bonus because Micronesia was considered a "hardship area"; she could save because there were no stores where she could spend her money, and with her savings she was putting her son through college in Hawaii.

Wives of officials find housekeeping easier because servants are cheap and plentiful. One mother of three children transplanted from a Chicago flat said, "I never used to have time to sit down. Now I can actually read a book."

When I commiserated Thelma Mackenzie of Majuro on her island exile, she retorted, "You needn't be sorry for us. It's wonderful. We've got it *made*."

This high-spirited attitude is partly genuine, partly a determination to make the best of things.

Comments one hears range all the way from "It's an awful bore" to "We have the most interesting and unusual work in the whole U.S. government service."

It cannot be denied that many of the American personnel come for the adventure of it; which is quite all right provided they really try to do a good job. Here is a golden opportunity to see something of the world. At the end of two years the staff member who elects to renew his contract is allowed three months off. If he chooses to go home he may travel there and back at Trust expense. Or he may prefer to journey at his own expense to some of the glamorous lands to the north, west, and south—Japan, Hong Kong, the Philippines, Malaysia, Bali, New Guinea, the Solomons, Australia, New Zealand, New Caledonia, Fiji. Or he may, sharing the expense with the Trust, go home and back the long way, visiting Vietnam, Thailand, Burma, India, Africa, and any or all of the countries of Europe.

Some prefer to take their vacation in paradise, wandering

through the island labyrinth, sailing the superb lagoons, enjoying some of the most thrilling deep-water fishing in the world, skin diving in the fantastic coral gardens, collecting tropical shells on beaches and reefs that have not already been picked over by a horde of tourists, exploring ruins and collecting artifacts left by a forgotten race, stopping on remote islands in the homes of warmhearted brown folk who still live in the golden age.

Or, if one is a loner, he may select any of a thousand uninhabited isles and make it his very own for three months, testing his powers of survival and self-sufficiency. What man is not boy enough to want to be a Robinson Crusoe? But in three months he'll be glad to get back to the comparatively mad whirl of one of the main islands.

The recluse would do better to stay in New York where he may occupy an apartment for ten or twenty years without exchanging a word with the people next door. Here there is none of the solitude of the great city. Your arrival, no matter who you are, is an event. Since a plane puts down only once or twice a week, there is bound to be a large reception committee. You will at once meet the Distad, a dozen or more of the American staff members, and the leading Micronesians. Your immediate difficulty will be to remember the faces and names of all who have been added so suddenly to your list of friends.

You are invited to attend a dinner party that very evening. You will please come at six. Perhaps your normal dinner hour is seven or seven-thirty and you are a bit surprised that these people should eat so early.

They don't. They sit around and talk with you and the other new arrivals, getting to know you, giving you a chance to know them. They are interested in you, and you find them interesting because of their varied personalities, their background, and the nature of their work, so radically different from any thing done by the average desk-bound executive in Chicago or Cleveland.

There are likely to be some fifty persons present. You meet every last one of them. The house, even if it is the Distad's, is too small for so many and those who prefer the fresh air sit on the porches or wander about the grounds. And everybody has a glass in his hand. In these islands liquor costs about one-third the price in the U.S.

"So cheap you can't afford *not* to drink," a judiciary secretary told us, and added, "I've never seen so much drinking as here."

This is one of the dividends the Trust offers to Americans who come for a term of duty in the islands. Sometimes the resulting befuddlement makes the dividend a deficit for both the individual and the government.

Yet, I must confess, we never saw anyone actually drunk. The drinks come one after another in steady succession. You did not need to fear a too-early dinner. An hour passes, and no dinner. Two hours. Three hours.

Between nine and ten there is the rattle of dishes. You pass a buffet table and take what you want. There are good American dishes and delightful island foods. You balance your plate on your knee and eat, drink, and talk.

After dinner there are after-dinner liqueurs. Tongues are well loosened by this time and you are on a first-name basis. Perhaps the party disbands at midnight, perhaps it goes on until two A.M.

However, there is a happy spirit of "do as you please." If you don't care to qualify for the degree of B.A. (Bachelor of Alcoholism) in this School of Hard Liquor, there are fruit juices and the refreshing liquid from a young coconut.

Not only are sociability and friendship easily available in the American community, but the Micronesians receive the stranger with a cordiality rare in this suspicious world. There is none of the sulky animosity that makes life for the white man rather less than pleasant in many parts of Africa, South America, Asia, where white presence is resented. Even in Europe the American does not always feel that he is being welcomed with open arms.

The Micronesians have not as yet taken to writing YANKS GO HOME! on the walls of public buildings.

The tale is told of one American with a timid and retiring nature who found the natives a little too friendly. Upon his arrival at the Royal Palauan Hotel he was given a quiet room near the rear entrance. This door was ordinarily kept locked to discourage girls of the town who had been in the habit of sneaking into the hotel to bed down with male guests.

On this night, however, someone had forgotten to lock it. A girl in quest of an hour's pleasure and a few American dollars slipped in and rapped on the door of the newcomer.

"What is it?" called the American.

"I come get your wash."

The guest climbed out of bed, turned on the light and looked at his watch. It was one A.M.

"You come for it in the morning," he suggested.

"No can. Only at night I wash."

Not wishing to lose the opportunity to have his laundry done, he opened the door and tried to use it as a shield, peering out from behind it. This effort at concealment was in vain. The girl smilingly closed the door and proceeded to undress.

"You go bed. I come quick."

Panic-stricken, he grabbed a sheet from the bed, flung it around him, and fled to the lobby.

He looked about for a lounge or davenport; he saw nothing but straight-backed chairs. He made himself uncomfortable in one of them and tried to compose his thoughts. If he waited awhile, she would go away.

After a quarter of an hour he crept down the hall to his room and looked in the keyhole. The room was dark. She had gone. He went in and, without turning on the light, crawled into bed. A pair of warm arms twined around his neck.

He escaped once more to the lobby. There the night watchman, after a good night's sleep, found him in the morning.

The incident is hardly typical. Most male exiles are not so insensitive to the charms of the brown sirens of the South Seas. There is no such freedom of action as in Tahiti, yet liaisons, temporary or permanent, between white and brown are not exceptional. Some formal marriages have taken place and have proved satisfactory.

At our first party in Palau, held in the home of Distad Francis Mahoney, we were received by a strikingly beautiful native girl who chattered gaily in perfect English and seemed as intelligent as she was vivacious.

"Who is she?" I asked the nearest available old-timer after she had gone to welcome other guests.

"Didn't you know? She's the Distad's wife. A princess. Daughter of one of the kings of Yap. Fine girl—they don't come better in any color."

"How long have they been married?"

"About twelve years. They have three sons."

"Twelve years. I didn't know anybody stayed that long."

"To Mahoney, this is home. He's one of the most valuable men in the Trust, because he knows so much about the natives. Being married to one helps him to understand them. He's anchored here, for good."

Not everyone stays so long. In fact the turnover is distressingly rapid. The personnel director has found that in the average year the turnover is 39 percent. Many leave for valid reasons, perhaps to put their children through school. Others leave just because they are constitutional tramps.

A drifter whom we shall not name had gone from job to job for thirty years and now found himself holding down a small assignment in the Trust. I asked him how he liked it.

"The only trouble," he said, "is that you have to stay two years."

Counting the days till one's time is up makes for poor service.

At the other extreme is John Spivey who has been on the job since the beginning, orienting with sage counsel every new Hicom as administrations come and go.

Another invaluable man is Dr. Aaron Jaffe who could not be cut off from his job except by a surgical operation.

As Director of Dental Services he trains native dentists and has supervision over their work throughout the entire Trust Territory. He is a little man with a heart as big as the three-million-square-mile range of his activities. At retirement age he is still as brisk as a new recruit. His father was a rabbi beloved on New York's East Side. The son finds the same satisfaction in service and his friends affectionately dub him "the Hebrew Albert Schweitzer."

He humorously recalls the difficult days of his childhood when his impecunious father used to take his five children on the streetcar, though there was no money in his pocket to pay the fare. Furtively the rabbi would pick up all the used transfers that had been dropped on the floor. When the conductor arrived to take the fare he would be handed the sheaf of transfers. By the time the bewildered official had leafed through the stack of papers only to find that they were all worthless, the six passengers would arrive at their destination and leave the car, the rabbi answering the conductor's protests with a meek "Me no speak English."

Jaffe's early privations have made him sensitive to the privations of others. His pockets bulge like the panniers of a donkey with candies for the children. At a native feast of island nobles he sat beside the chief, who stacked the honored guest's plate high with food. When no one was watching, Dr. Jaffe passed the plate back to hungry children huddled behind the circle of the elite. Presently the plate was returned to him, empty. The chief, observing the bare plate, filled it again mountain high. Again he noticed in a few moments that it was empty. When this had happened three times, the chief gazed at the small doctor in amazement and said:

"Little man—big appetite!"

Dr. Jaffe not only teaches but practices, and with apparent inconsistency charges five cents for a filling on one island and twenty-five cents on another.

Upon landing he goes to the trading company and asks, "How much did you pay the people for their copra this year?"

Suppose the total is a thousand dollars and there are a thousand people on the island—that's one dollar a person. So Dr. Jaffe fixes his price very low. On another island where earnings were five times as much, his price goes up accordingly. Of course he never charges what it costs.

A naval officer said to Jaffe, "I suppose you don't use the best materials for these people."

Jaffe was indignant. "I would use the best for you—why not for them?"

He tells his native dentists when they turn in records of the number of treatments given, "You can't impress me with quantity. I don't want fifty poor fillings. I want one good filling."

Many other members of the American staff are quite as conscientious, though perhaps not so picturesque, as "the Hebrew Albert Schweitzer."

How do they compare with their Japanese predecessors?

It would be pleasant to be able to say that the American staff is in every way superior. But I clearly remember several Japanese Albert Schweitzers—doctors, administrators, teachers, businessmen—who would go far out of their way to help a "native." Often they did not think of the islanders as "natives," sharply distinct from themselves.

This was natural, since Japanese blood is partly Micronesian.

It would be too simple to say that racial affinity always meant better treatment. Besides the Japanese Albert Schweitzers, there were Japanese of lesser stature who were all the more harsh and domineering because they were at pains to prove that they were of quite a different breed from the islanders, and far superior. They balanced unsteadily on their pedestals. If they did not get what they considered due respect, they got tough.

The American does not worry so much about respect. He doesn't feel he has to prove anything. Perhaps it is smugness; perhaps it is the reasonable knowledge that there is something in his own ancestry and his own civilization that gives him a special place in the sun. His attitude is paternal, not fraternal. Brothers may fight; a good parent doesn't need to. Whatever the reason, there is no record of a native having been struck or otherwise physically abused by an American official.

We are no altruists. We did not take over Micronesia to help the Micronesians. We took it for military reasons—to strengthen our position in the western Pacific. The Japanese were there for exactly the same purpose, plus one other. The secondary purpose was to populate the islands with Japanese and make the area an integral part of the Japanese Empire. We have no such ambition. We can afford, as the Japanese could not, to encourage native self-expression and self-government. Inside the bases, we are selfish. Outside, we are there to serve the island people.

The chance to serve is attractive to many persons, as witness the success of the Peace Corps.

Bud Bonavito, an Italian-born New Yorker on Yap, said, "Over here, when I do a job I can feel I'm helping somebody. Back home, a job is usually just a case of a guy trying to make a buck for himself."

It's particularly satisfying if one can help someone else and make a buck at the same time. Salaries for Trust personnel run from $5,000 to $15,000, plus 25 percent as a "post differential." House, medical care, transportation to and from the homeland, public transport on the island, are free. Liquor and cigarettes are nominally priced, and food, with certain exceptions, is good and cheap. Said a housewife on Truk, "Considering the great distance that things had to be shipped, we had a fantastic assortment, all kinds of canned and prepared foods, things I'd never seen back home—English biscuits and chocolates, Danish cheeses, Dutch candies, all the frozen vegetables and fruits, and TV dinners, including Cornish hens, chicken livers, turkeys, and tenderloins."

This abundance does not prevail on all islands. But where incoming shipments are few, and more costly, one may always turn to the island-grown fruits, vegetables, meats, and the bounty of the sea.

Along with the advantages go many disadvantages, privations, hardships. But balancing all of them is the inward content of doing something to help people who need help, and appreciate it. Many staff members upon leaving for home have felt as Judge Toomin did. He wrote later in his fascinating memoirs, *Black Robe and Grass Skirt*:

> I was most deeply aware of the strong emotional bond I had developed with the people in this Micronesian paradise. As we taxied off to our place at the top of the runway and passed the arms waving farewell on our quick take-off, I was unable to resist the hot tears.

Anything that will bring hot tears to the eyes of a judge must have merit.

19.

It's Better

OUR position was peculiar, since we were the only American visitors who had seen this island world under both regimes, Japanese and American.

So we got the same query everywhere from earnest Distads and staff members:

"Is it better now, or worse?"

It was impossible to offer a glib answer. We had to reply equivocally, "Better and worse."

In some respects the Americans are doing a far better job than their predecessors.

❦

It used to be said that the Micronesians were a dying race. They were being decimated by the guns, liquor, and diseases brought in by white traders, pirates, and adventurers. It was not uncommon for a sea captain offended by some native chief to put ashore a sailor suffering from smallpox or measles, causing an epidemic that wiped out most of the population.

The people of Yap, long considered a dying race, have doubled in number since World War II.

This is good progress, considering the difficulty of making the Yapese take modern medicine seriously. They are still inclined to believe that illness is caused by the cantankerous spirit of some ancestor, angry because he has not had adequate respect from the living. Instead of repairing at once to the hospital they seek out the fortune-teller (*tobey*) to learn what they have to do to satisfy the disgruntled ghost. Those who do go to the hospital and fail to get prompt relief also fall easy prey to the fortune-teller.

A man of Yap called Bazgiz suffered a chronic ailment for five years and visited the hospital time after time, each time obtaining only temporary relief. At last he turned to the tobey. That worthy advised him that his name was the cause of the trouble. It was the name of one of his ancestors. A rival ancestor, Giltaman, was jealous. If the sick man would take the name Giltaman he would recover.

The change was made, Bazgiz became Giltaman, the hospital visits that had been keeping him alive were discontinued. Within a year he was dead.

In other districts where there is somewhat less sorcery and more confidence in modern treatment, infant mortality has declined and life expectancy increased. The net result is that in the Trust Territory as a whole the native population, 40,000 at the end of the Japanese regime, has climbed in the short span of twenty years to 80,000. This remarkable recovery has been encouraging, and alarming. Overpopulation has raised its ominous head. On Ponape births outnumber deaths seven to one.

The rate of growth in continental United States is 1.8 percent. Contrast this with 3.5 percent in the Marshalls, 5 percent in the Palaus, 5.7 percent in Kusaie, 7.3 percent in the Marianas—and an overall figure of 3.9 percent in the Trust Territory as a whole. An investigating Yale University professor of geography, examining this "extremely high rate of natural in-

crease," calculates grimly, "In terms of island land for food production, these rates, if continued, could truly be described as
explosive."

This rather frightening improvement is due to many factors:
better medical facilities, better nutrition, better sanitation, im-
munization programs, a stronger will to live.

"Medical care is much better than in Japanese times," we
were told by Koichi Sana, Truk Hospital Administrator, himself part Japanese. "There were no Micronesian doctors then. If
a native needed an operation he was just out of luck. Japanese
requiring operations were taken to Japan. Natives just died."

Sana took us through the Truk hospital. It was larger than
the previous structure, and perhaps a little better. Screens were
broken, admitting mosquitoes and flies. Cobwebs hung in corners. Bandages and surgical dressings lay in heaps. The native
staff was a bit careless, but earnest and devoted.

Sana admitted that Americans on Truk were not enthusiastic
about the hospital. They came to be treated for minor ailments
but if it was anything serious they flew to the Navy Hospital on
Guam.

The hospital on Yap is worse. But on Majuro and Palau we
were heartened by the cleanliness and air of efficiency of brand-
new cement-block hospitals almost the equals of those to be
found in the average American small town.

On the principle that medical services are appreciated more
if they cost something, nominal fees are charged. Hospitaliza-
tion costs fifty cents a day. Minor operations are performed for
a dollar, major operations for ten dollars or less. Outpatient
calls are made for ten cents to twenty-five cents. A fellow traveler on one of our flights was an eye specialist who was making
a 300-mile round trip to do a single cataract operation. The fee
would be waived since the patient was unable to pay.

The visitor is shocked to learn that in all the islands there is not a single native M.D. But this is not as serious as it sounds. There are many "medical practitioners" (they would be called "medical officers" in British islands) who have had four years of training in the Central Medical School in Fiji, but do not technically rate the degree of M.D. because they went to medical school direct from high school rather than by way of college. The Trust Territory has no college. Yet these men are qualified physicians and are highly respected by the few American doctors who work with them.

Native dentists are taking over under the inspired Dr. Jaffe, Director of Dental Services. In 1958 there were five American dentists in the Trust Territory. In 1964 there was only one, Dr. Jaffe himself, but twenty Micronesian dentists were practicing in the territory and eighteen more were in training.

Next in rank below the medical practitioners and dentists are the "health aides." They are trained by the Health Department to give simple treatments and conduct local dispensaries. In the Truk Islands alone there are forty-five dispensaries presided over by health aides. Because of the sometimes rough physical conditions in the out islands, all health aides are men. They even deliver babies, though twenty years ago it would have been inconceivable that a man should look upon a woman in childbirth. The traditional ignorant and unclean midwife is now on her way out.

Important in the medical setup are the expert crews of "sanitarians" who clean up villages and teach the people how to keep them clean. This program was initiated by the Japanese, but it was then more a matter of compulsion than persuasion. The police were trained to act as sanitarians and authorized to punish offenders.

"I can't sneeze without the *junke* [policeman] making a notch in his stick," complained one native.

Through such watchfulness, distressing as it might be to the individual, epidemics were reported and checked almost before they began. Sanitary conditions were forcibly mended. "Model houses" were built. The Japanese government paid one-half the cost of construction, then dictated what should be done. The roof must not be of thatch, but of corrugated iron (farewell to romance!). There must be real windows and doors. The floor must be raised a meter from the ground so that air might pass freely beneath it, but not through it. It must be a solid floor, not a sieve. And there must be beds for sleeping.

"Why," I asked the Japanese, "when you yourselves sleep on the floor?"

"But the native floor is not clean."

The new houses were a serious artistic loss. They were iron-lidded wooden boxes on stilts. Modern clothing, demanded by the police, was not only less attractive but less healthful than the former clothing or lack of it. Clothes soaked by rain or sea spray were allowed to dry on the body, causing respiratory ailments. In the western Carolines there was bitter resistance to the new rules. On a cold day the man who owned a pair of trousers might use it as a shawl, the legs tied under the chin. School children were given clothes and required to wear them in the classroom; which they obediently did, then left them in their desks.

The sanitarians of today, with no authority except that of common sense, are more successful—if not in housing, at least in village cleanup. The able native Assistant Director of Sanitation, Nachse Siren, tells us how such a project was carried out in the Truk village of Onongoch.

"The people were friendly and cooperative. Above all they were interested in improving the sanitation, health and appearance of their village.

"The place had no garbage disposal, no pigpens, few toilet facilities, and many flies and mosquitoes.

"The team planned a program in which the people could participate. Since few had money for lumber or tin, the use of native materials was stressed. It was encouraging to see the people build benjos, pigpens and even covers for water wells from native materials. It cost them nothing except a little time and work to have sanitary facilities of which they could be proud. While the men built six new benjos, the women wove grass covers to go on the wells. The community joined in digging garbage-burial pits. We introduced mosquito-destroying fish called *gambusia*. We provided insecticides to kill flies and mosquitoes and the villagers worked to get rid of the breeding places.

"The village is not perfect, but it is now clean and presentable. The people were honored by having the U.S. Congressional party and the High Commissioner visit their village to observe the results of this program. Both parties were pleased with what they saw and the Onongoch people were proud that their efforts were rewarded. They put on canoe races, dances, and a feast for the visitors after the latter had inspected the village."

In the territory as a whole, yaws used to be a major menace. During the past fifteen years the incidence of yaws has been reduced to one half of one percent. Leprosy is almost unknown. Smallpox has disappeared. The import of narcotic drugs is banned and there is no known case of addiction in the Trust Territory. There are few if any alcoholics. There is no law against prostitution and none is necessary since there is no prostitution.

The conquest of tuberculosis is less satisfactory. Early cases can be cured in three months by isomycin and streptomycin. But in islands seldom visited early cases become late before they can be treated. A young and vigorous American doctor resigned his post as Assistant Medical Administrator and left the Trust in bitter protest against the neglect of the urgent medical needs of the vast majority of the two thousand Micronesian islands. The drugs are available, and the native medicos; the bottleneck is transportation.

The greatest dangers to health come from outside the island world.

"Every time a ship comes in," said a doctor on Majuro, "you can expect that about two weeks later the islanders will come down with something, generally a 'cold' but a different kind each time. A ship with two cases of mumps put in. Result, eighty-six cases of mumps on this island. A new District Administrator arrived with flu. Result, four thousand cases of flu. One of the flu patients slipped away to the atoll of Arno, twenty miles distant. Result, eight hundred cases of flu on Arno."

Other troubles come in tins.

"A steady intake of canned foods," says a Distad, "results in deficiencies which manifest themselves in neuritis and a propensity to respiratory diseases. When a few people catch colds on Ebeye, it is only a matter of hours before most of the village is down with colds. This is due, perhaps, to an inability to resist infection due to improper diet."

Lectures, motion pictures, and demonstrations are used to persuade the islanders that American ways are not necessarily the best in all respects and to encourage a return to some of the foods to be found fresh on the atolls and in the sea. With all its defects and drawbacks, the health program of the Trust is enlightened and progressive.

Not only the body, but the mind has a better chance now.

The Spanish did nothing, except through their church missions, to educate young Micronesia. The German government had only one school functioning when the Japanese arrived in

1914. By 1936 the Japanese government of the islands had twenty-five schools for natives in operation. There are today nearly three hundred.

The Japanese quite naturally thought first of their own people. A native student on Ponape got five years of schooling, a Japanese twelve.

Today the eager student, *if* he lives in one of the main islands, may go through elementary school, intermediate school, high school, and stands a chance of getting a scholarship which will carry him through Guam College or the University of Hawaii.

But the largest word in the preceding sentence is *if*. The Trust Territory is divided into six districts, and on the main island of each district is a high school. That means six high schools for two thousand islands scattered over three million square miles of sea. Transportation being what it is, or is not, some 98 percent of young people of high school age never darken the door of a high school.

College, except for a favored few, is "out." There is no provision whatever for education beyond high school within the Trust. A teacher in the Ponape High School told us:

"There are only fifteen college graduates in the Trust Territory. If there were the same proportion as in the United States we would have 760."

The theory in regard to higher education in the Trust has been like that of the Belgians in the Congo: concentrate on primary schools. The Congo result was that with the dawn of independence there were only sixteen college graduates in that vast and unwieldy nation. In a land without leaders it is no wonder that independence was followed by turmoil, massacre, and cannibalism.

Even the three hundred primary schools of the Trust are woefully inadequate. The annual report of the territory is not intended to be a joke book, yet the author of the section in Educational Advancement must have had his tongue in his cheek when he wrote: "Compulsory school attendance for all children between seven and thirteen years is required."

You cannot compel children to go to a school that does not exist. Even in such populous areas as the Truk lagoon only a handful of the 245 islands have schools. Going to school by canoe is theoretically possible but practically impossible during bad weather or during harvest periods when parents are too busy to transport children not old enough to paddle their own canoe.

Even on a large Truk island such as Tol where it should be possible to walk to school, home and school may be separated by a dozen miles with no connection but a neglected and over-grown path made almost impassable by rocks, bogs, and fallen trees. The student, if he succeeds in surmounting all the obstacles, arrives in such a state of exhaustion that he is in no condition to absorb any knowledge from teachers or books. It is admitted that at least 40 percent of Truk children of school age are not in school. In hundreds of out islands the proportion of absentees would be much closer to 100 percent.

Compulsory, indeed.

There have, however, been improvements in the curriculum. Some of these are built on good foundations laid by the Japanese. Nipponese teachers made a point of training islanders for life in their own islands. But as international tension grew, they were constrained by higher authorities to teach emperor worship, discredit the white man's civilization, and proclaim the coming of the "Greater East Asia Co-Prosperity Sphere" or, in plainer language, a Japan-enslaved Orient.

The present program is at least free of any such political contamination. The mistakes that have been made have been honest mistakes. One has been that if the natives want educa-

tion they should get it by their own efforts, build their own
schools, employ their own teachers and pay for them out of
their own lava-lavas.

But how can you expect primitives who know nothing of
formal education to realize its value? The Japanese did not expect it, and the government not only built the schools and paid
the teachers, but supplied books, pencils, clothing, and sometimes food as well. The cost of native education to the government was more than four times the total of the poll tax received
from natives.

The postwar administration has now belatedly been ordered
by Washington to return to the policy of its predecessor. The
change has been welcomed by the new High Commissioner,
who reports in 1964:

> Formerly, the support of elementary education was made al-
> most completely the responsibility of the local community.
> The result, except for a few good schools built under a grant-
> in-aid program, was inadequate and deteriorated elementary
> school buildings, limited school equipment, and poorly trained
> and poorly paid teachers. The present accelerated program
> will result in modern schools, good school equipment, ample
> school supplies, and trained U.S. and Micronesian teachers.

There is still plenty for the local folk to do. They help put
up the school building, make furniture, pay something toward
maintenance, but they have the support and backing of the
higher powers.

There has been another fundamental change, one that would
make the anthropologists of 1945 turn in their graves. These
gentlemen recommended, with the best humanitarian motives,
that all education be in the native languages. They had nothing
but contempt for Japan's insistence that teaching be in the Jap-

anese language. They suspected Japan of conspiring to Japanize the islanders, violate the terms of the League of Nations Mandate, and keep the islands as a permanent appendage of Japan.

In all these suspicions they were, of course, quite right. But their conclusions as to what should be done were quite wrong. They decided that out of respect for the cultural traditions of the native he should be taught to speak, read, and write the native language.

But there is no native language. Or, rather, there is a different language for the natives of every island. Saipan cannot understand Yap; nor Yap, Palau; nor Palau, Truk; nor Truk, Ponape; nor Ponape, Kusaie; nor Kusaie, Majuro.

Democratic unity is of course impossible with such a diversity of tongues. If every state in the American Union spoke a different language we should probably have fifty nations instead of one.

A localized language stunts mental growth. Few of the islanders read. It would be of little use at present to learn, because there would be nothing to read (except, on some islands, the Bible, translated by the missionaries). No commercial publisher could be persuaded to print newspapers, magazines, and books in a language read by only a few hundred or a few thousand people. It would not pay. Hence a literature in an island language is impossible. The natives' only hope to tap the knowledge of the world is to learn a language in which the world's knowledge is published.

Another consideration: the Palau language contains only six thousand words, the Truk language three thousand, the Yap language only one thousand. The English language includes well over 600,000 terms. A few eating and sleeping words did well enough in the isolated tropical isle. But times have changed. Making shift with a small coconut vocabulary in this modern, complex world into which the native has been introduced would be like paddling a canoe in a motorboat race.

New words make new horizons. The mind is expanded as it finds new ways of expression.

But, objected the anthropologists who were called in to advise the Administration, if you teach in English you will be charged by your critics with linguistic imperialism. Even if we grant that a world language should be taught, why should it be English? It is not the only world language.

How about Japanese, of which the islanders already have some knowledge?

Japanese is a very difficult and exceedingly provincial language. Spoken Japanese is fairly simple, but written Japanese, since it uses Chinese ideographs, is one of the most bewildering languages on earth. It is not used to any considerable extent elsewhere on this planet.

Chinese is equally difficult, and for the same reason. The Russian language is split into dialects. French, the "diplomatic" language, is spoken by some 70,000,000 persons, German by 98,-000,000, Spanish by 150,000,000. The English language is spoken by 300,000,000 people.

English is pre-eminently the language of world communication. According to figures presented by the National Geographic Society, three-fourths of the world's letters are written in English, half of the world's newspapers are in English, announcers for three-fifths of the earth's radio stations broadcast in English. Its use is more widely distributed over the world than that of any other language.

Moreover, as Christopher Hollis has said, "The English language is the language, far more than any other, in which the story of freedom is told." That is of importance if we look forward to ultimate democracy in the Pacific islands.

Certainly all that is good in native culture should be preserved. The history, geography, agriculture, and handicrafts of the island world have been taught in Micronesian schools, and will be. The native languages will continue to be used in homes. There has been and should be no effort to suppress Micronesia's scores of languages and dialects.

But the need for some more comprehensive language is apparent. Island languages are severely limited. They make no provision for the thousands of new ideas of a changing world.

These facts dawned only slowly upon the bureaucratic mind. As late as 1959 the Trust annual report declared:

> The mother tongue of the peoples shall be the language through or by means of which instruction shall be carried on in the elementary schools.

The missions, both Catholic and Protestant, never subscribed to this policy and commonly taught in English beginning with the first grade. The Micronesians themselves through the Council of Micronesia petitioned for teaching in English. President Kennedy in one of the last acts of a brief and golden career ordered the change in administration policy and today all teaching is supposed to be in English. I say "supposed to be" since many Micronesian teachers cannot—as yet—speak English. They must speedily acquire the ability to use it, or be replaced. More than two hundred American teachers have been brought in to tutor them and work with them in the classrooms.

The two Kennedy-inspired changes, firm government responsibility for education and the adoption of a world language, bring a new wind into the doldrums of island education. The effect will not be immediate. A half century hence when those now beginning their education have reached the age of wisdom, the full impact of these changes will be felt.

20.

It's Worse

IN some important respects the Americans could profitably take lessons from the Nipponese and their thirty years of trial and error.

This goes against the grain. We like to think we bring a magic touch to anything we undertake. We have been constitutionally critical of all the great colonizers, Spain and Portugal in South America, Britain in India, Holland in the Indies, France in Africa, Japan in the Pacific. Now these venerable colonialists have a chance to sit back and watch our juvenile performance in one of the last colonies left on the face of the earth.

In health and education we are not doing badly. That leaves out material prosperity. Perhaps idealists will say that material prosperity is not important.

The islander without a job, without money, without the decent house he once had, without the running water, electricity, lights, heater, cooler, radio, refrigerator, washing machine, flush toilet, that he sees in the houses of his white friends, will not agree that material prosperity is of no consequence.

The Micronesian, at least in the populous district centers, is well out of the fish and coconut era, yet not in the modern age. He stands on one foot in the doorway, unable to go back or forward.

He progressed rapidly under the Japanese. True, this progress was not always voluntary. He was compelled to be industrious, compelled to earn, forced to have money in his pocket.

"We prefer Americans," a Yapese remarked, "because the Japanese made us work."

The native anthropologist Defngin pinpointed the present difficulty in three words:

"Too much freedom!"

"You are too easy with the natives," said Carlos Etscheit, Belgian planter on Ponape. "The Japanese made them carry two-hundred-pound bags of copra. Americans put copra in hundred-pound bags and the natives complain it's too heavy."

One of the island kings of Yap, old and wise, put it this way:

"We have been pauperized by generosity. Your Navy began it. They gave the people everything they asked for. They thoroughly spoiled us. Now it's hard to get back on a self-supporting basis. What is most needed is not handouts, but cooperation at the village level. The Americans all live in fine houses in town—they seldom get out into the country. If you would imitate your Peace Corps and go out, some of you, and actually live in a jungle village, put up a really attractive native-style house for yourselves, using local materials, and beautify the grounds, and show by actual example how farms and vegetable gardens can be improved and local industries created, you would do more for us than you can sitting behind your desks in town."

Persons who used to have jobs during Japanese times and

have none now still hang around the once-active administrative centers, and live in huts of shreds and patches, Micronesia's first slums. They have become slum-minded. They look enviously at the good things in store windows, but don't enter the store.

A Ponapean merchant in his empty shop lamented, "This used to be a busy place. There were many customers and they had real money to spend. Not now."

The per capita income of the Micronesian is estimated by headquarters to be $58 a year. During the heyday of the Japanese it was approximately five times this figure.

An investigating commission of the Pacific Science Board has made this report:

> The interests of both Germans and Japanese in economic development and research led to an expanding economy for islanders as well as foreign residents, although the islanders remained at the bottom of the heap. The low economic value of the islands to the United States makes it seem unlikely that the real income of the islanders will easily regain its heights of the Japanese period. A certain amount of disillusionment of the islanders with the idea of economic progress has been inevitable under the Americans. Economic progress is still held desirable but conceived to be nearly impossible to attain.

The annual report of the Hicom for 1960 noted that imports for the year amounted to $3,030,745 while exports totaled only $1,722,336. The Japanese reversed the order, exports far outstripping imports. The exports of one island alone, Saipan, exceeded the present exports of the entire Trust.

The Japanese used (and abused) the islands. We merely neglect them. The innumerable industries that were created have died on the vine. There were fish canneries that employed hundreds of Micronesians. There were factories to turn trochus shell into buttons. There were processing plants for coconut fiber. There were lively cottage industries that turned the strong leaves of pandanus and palm into woven goods for an eager Japanese market. There were handicrafts of many kinds—they still exist to a small extent but are discouraged by high United States tariffs that bar them from such mass outlets as American department stores. Timber was cut, bauxite was mined. Now there is no work for lumberjacks or miners. Buried treasure to the value of a million dollars a year was dug up by the Japanese on the single island of Angaur. That this buried treasure was not bullion or pieces of eight, but bird droppings, did not detract from its value.

Guano, rich in phosphate, has for ages been industriously laid down by birds on the flat coral island of Angaur. Possibly two million years were required to do the job, since the deposits are forty feet deep. Before the war it was being mined at the rate of seventy thousand tons a year.

It went to Japan for use as fertilizer to perform the favorite Japanese trick of magic, making one acre do the work of twenty.

The treasure hunt was not difficult. No mine shafts or tunnels deep underground were necessary. The phosphate lay on the surface. One had only to remove the trees and shrubs, then break up the precious material with a pick and load it into dump cars. Small locomotives hauled the cars to the drying house. There the phosphate rode an endless belt which dropped it little by little into a great revolving cylinder twelve feet in diameter and sixty feet long where hot air from a coal furnace thoroughly dried the material. Another belt carried it away to a storage shed. When a ship arrived the phosphate took another belt journey up a fantastic bridge projecting over the sea high enough to clear a ship's superstructure and fell through a mammoth tube into the ship's hatches.

The workmen came on a six-month contract. Alone—no wives or children were allowed; the island was too small. Many

Micronesians were eager to come, for the pay was good. Some who were not so eager were "persuaded."

Their women wept when they left, for Angaur had an evil reputation thanks to native tradition. It had long been known as the Island of the Dead. Its rather unearthly guano waste was thought to be the promenade of ghosts. Angaur was a sort of purgatory. The dead came here to be tested for an indefinite period after which those who qualified were taken to heaven, called *Babluades* or "The Village Over Us." Angaur was thought to be a place of terrible agony of spirit in the uncertainty as to whether heaven or hell was to be one's final destination. When a person was mentally distressed it was said that he was suffering Angaur. These native beliefs did not make employment on the island any more agreeable.

The laborers lived on shelves in a long wooden shed like a loggers' bunkhouse but not so comfortable—yet much more airy, light, and sanitary than the average jungle hut. After hours they played pool, ping-pong, and table games in a dingy clubhouse. But their lives were dreary, womanless and homeless. Nevertheless they did earn, and saved what they earned, for there was no place to spend it. At the end of six months they returned to their rejoicing families with plenty of money to exchange in the numerous shops for Japanese goods at prices ridiculously low as compared with those for similar articles in America or Europe.

Now Angaur is truly the island of the dead, the jungle has recovered the man-made scars, and millions of dollars' worth of treasure lies undisturbed. To re-establish the industry would take money, and that is not available.

℣

"Islands of little account" was the description brought back by explorers soon after Spain had acquired the islands. They remained of little account during Spanish rule. The Germans, with their flair for scientific agriculture, began to turn them to account. The Japanese multiplied this effort many hundreds of times and accomplished nothing short of an economic revolution in the Micronesian archipelago.

In nothing else does the genius of the Japanese people show to greater advantage than in agriculture. They have been trained for the conquest of the soil in their own tight islands. The Spaniards surveying barren Saipan could hardly foresee rich plantations of sugarcane twenty feet high billowing in the breeze.

One of the finest sugarcanes in the world was developed here. Java cane was formerly used. Unsatisfied scientists blended it with other canes from all over the world, producing endless varieties. The final result of this polygamy was the birth of a remarkable half-caste, a blend of Java and Formosa, which throve in the soil of Saipan. It grew to great size, had high sugar content, and yielded six million dollars' worth of sugar a year.

The Japanese sugar executives gave the same unremitting attention to their job that their misguided militarist brothers devoted to the science of war. The manager of the Saipan sugar mill spoke to me in good English and explained that he had been in all the sugar countries and had worked for years in a sugar mill in Cuba.

Now there is no more cane on Saipan and talented sugar executives are producing wealth elsewhere.

Other "islands of little account" were converted by the Japanese into vast coconut plantations and the copra (dried kernel of the coconut) took rank with the world's best. The Japanese stood ready to give any copra farmer an iron roof, free of charge, to put on his drying house in place of the thatch roof. Under the latter, the wind dries the copra in about ten days.

When iron is used the wind is supplemented by the sun's heat beating upon the roof, and the copra dries in five days.

How to use barren uplands was a hard problem. Apparently just nothing would grow there. Not because of lack of rain; there was plenty of that. The good soil was washed into the sea. Many plants would not tolerate such a drenching. What would flourish in poor soil, and at the same time defy the downpour?

The answer was tapioca. Wild specimens of it were found here and there growing to tree size. But they contained only 16 percent starch. World-ranging Japanese for the agricultural department fixed upon Java tapioca and brought it back to Micronesia. It yielded 35 percent starch. Large plantations were put in, mills were built to grind the roots into a white powder, and the cake and confection industry of the world bought all the tapioca Micronesia could produce.

The Spaniards had nothing but contempt for the pineapples that grew wild on some of the islands. They were dry, woody, and tasteless. But they did grow. That was enough for the planners from Nippon—they introduced improved varieties and encouraged native farmers by offering a reward of ten yen for every hectare planted to pineapples and cared for for two years.

Palauans were feverishly raising pigs, for the government would not only lend animals for breeding purposes but reward the farmer with six yen for every pig born. In the same way, goats, cows, and chickens carried prices on their heads. Cattle raising was introduced by a young Japanese who brought thirty cattle from Japan. Most of them died. He bought better cattle and managed to make them thrive and calve. He accumulated one hundred, the largest herd at that time in the South Sea Islands. Cattle raising has now lapsed in importance except on one island, Saipan.

The Japanese even developed islands that the casual observer would consider hopeless. Rich soil was actually sent by the shipload to the barren coral atolls of the Marshalls. On certain rocky islands a tree known as the *soshiju*, from Formosa, was planted. It twines its roots around a rock and grows thirty feet high in three years. Its falling leaves and decaying logs make a soil where almost none existed. Of course it is a long-term project. When I asked the Palau agricultural director how long, he replied brightly, as if promising something for tomorrow morning before breakfast, "I think we will have these islands fit for farming in one hundred years."

But he went on to point out that a century is a brief period when you consider the untold ages these islands have been lying unused and useless.

Phosphate from Angaur regenerated the land on other islands. Another pulmotor for exhausted soil was the lemon hibiscus. Yam growing tires out the soil in ten years. But it was found that if the fast-growing hibiscus was allowed to perforate the hard dry ground with its labyrinth of roots, within a few months there was light rich soil ready for another decade of service.

One problem, ever present in the tropics, was to keep the jungle out of the garden. It crawls in, smothering everything with weeds and creepers. But it cannot get through a vigorous thicket of bamboo. So the government, while preparing the land for farming, shut out the jungle with walls of feathery bamboo.

All these imaginative projects and experiments were effectively wiped out by war. The new proprietors had to begin again under the heavy handicaps of postwar disorder, a discouraged people, and limited funds. A real beginning has been made, as noted in the chapters on Ponape and Truk. This beginning, however, has taken twenty years, and is limited to a few islands. In many areas instead of the progress that might have been expected there has been further stagnation.

When we turn from the soil to the sea, the picture is worse.

"The possibilities of the islands are limited," said Governor-General Hayashi, "of the sea unlimited."

Most of the three million square miles of Micronesia is sea, not land. Nearly all varieties of fish may be found here, most of them in abundance. The Japanese were keenly aware of the treasures of the sea. Micronesian marine products earned seven million dollars a year. Most of the export went to Japan, but from there much was relayed to all parts of the world. Japanese canned tuna entering the United States caused not a little worry to the fishing industry on the Pacific Coast.

First among the marine products of the southern sea was bonito. Daily peril was the lot of the bonito fisherman. He must go outside the reef, in the open sea. He could not wait for good weather. In waves that would shake an ocean liner his small boat dropped like a descending elevator into the hollows and was tossed skyward on the crests.

The Japanese supplanted the canoes with motorboats. These were not much safer than the great canoes, being only some forty feet in length. But they were much better for bonito fishing, since they were able to go rapidly to the point where the school of fish might be seen leaping from the sea, too preoccupied in fighting among themselves to notice the approach of the swift craft.

The hooks were sometimes baited with sardines, sometimes with feathers! But the best bait of all proved to be the gasoline motor.

The sound of the motor brought the fish. The government was so eager to develop bonito fishing that it would provide a motorboat free of charge to any group of thirty or forty Japanese who would undertake fishing. The men then owned the boat jointly and carried on work as an association.

The history of the bonito after capture was rather amazing. In a shore processing plant, the fish was boiled, then the head cut off, and the body cut longitudinally into four. It was turned over to operators armed with tweezers and every bone was pulled. The deboned fish was dried over fire for a few days and smoked for two weeks. Then girls manicured off the rough, smoky exterior with sharp knives until the fish took on the appearance of polished red mahogany.

It was stuck away in damp sheds to mildew. The mildew gave it that choice tang. When it was thoroughly blotched with the gray growth, the mildew was wiped off and the fish was sunned, only to mildew again. For the best results this process was repeated from three to five times. Thenceforth the fish would be practically immune from mildew. It would keep indefinitely. There are said to be pieces one hundred years old. Many stores in Japan offer pieces ten or twelve years old. Like wine, it improves with age.

It is as hard as wood. To the foreign visitor in a Japanese store, a tubful of *katsuobushi* (as it is called) looks like a collection of clubs or blackjacks, the purpose of which it is difficult to imagine.

The Japanese pay a high price for katsuobushi and one piece will last the average family many months. It is used as a flavoring rather than as a food. Thin shavings of it are put into the daily soup. Foreigners in Japan have learned its value and its use has been extended to America and Europe. Its manufacture might well be revived, for a little publicity would make a ready sale for it in many countries.

Deep-sea fishing was turned by the Japanese from a casual adventure into a huge commercial industry. The prevailing method of fishing was by long line. The line might be as much as seventy miles long—yes, I said seventy—and from it depended eighteen hundred vertical lines ending in hooks. The ship—large, fast and costly—began to draw in lines at about two P.M. The main take was tuna. But there would also be marlin, jumping high in the air in a burst of spray and appearing to walk on their tails; or sailfish, streaking along the surface in a flash of color, then raising their sails and reversing their course at full speed; or swordfish, angrily plunging their swords against the steel hull.

The line hauling, begun at two, might continue until midnight. Then the crew turned in until 3:30 A.M. when the rebaiting of the hooks must begin.

This went on for two to four days until the ship was topheavy with uncounted tons of fish and must return to port to unload.

So it was, and is no longer. The huge export of marine products from Micronesia has been succeeded by import—of fish in cans.

Today a serious attempt is being made to revive the fishing industry. We saw a seagoing fishing boat under construction in Truk, and one is in service at Palau. But to build the necessary fleet of several dozen such vessels and construct the necessary cold storage facilities would require money that at present is not in sight.

What the government cannot do, private industry can. And now that a changed policy allows the entry of private business, large American fish packers have come in to build ships and processing plants.

Buttons were big business in the Japanese Nanyo. Iridescent shells brought up by divers were transformed into gleaming mother-of-pearl buttons for women's clothing in England or America. The plastic button became a serious competitor, but in the last ten years there has been a revival of interest in the lustrous button of mother-of-pearl. Within the Trust, nothing is being done to satisfy this demand.

These waters were educated to yield pearl as well as mother-of-pearl. Ten thousand pearls a year came from Palau to the jewelry cases of Japan and the West. These were the famous Mikimoto cultured pearls. They could in no sense be called imitation pearls, for they were thoroughly genuine. But the oysters which made them were encouraged—subsidized—by man. Because of this encouragement the pearls could be produced in great numbers and were therefore much cheaper than accidental pearls. They were, however, identical in composition and in beauty.

The difference was only this: an oyster adventuring on its own might pick up a bit of shell or stone, and, unable to expel the irritating fragment, would cover it with a lustrous, calcareous concretion, thus gradually forming a pearl. But for every oyster that experienced this fate, ten thousand might escape it. At the pearl farm, laboratory experts opened oysters and introduced a bit of shell into each, so that every oyster would produce a pearl.

From that moment on, it was up to the oyster. The process was exactly the same as in the case of the accidental pearl. The annoying bit of foreign matter was sheathed in layer after layer of pearl. The gem was completed in from three to four years (half the time required in the Japan pearl farms where the water was colder). During these years the oysters were kept in wire cages suspended in the lagoon.

When the oyster had had time to do its work it was taken into the laboratory and the pearl extracted.

There was nothing artificial about the pearl. Even the particle at its center was the same sort of fragment that might be picked up by an oyster from the sea. But since a vain world pays for its gems, not according to their beauty but according to the difficulty of getting them, the accidental pearl will always cost more than the cultured.

The Palau gems were of unusual size, many of them from a quarter inch to a half inch in diameter. Most were white. Rarer and therefore more costly ones were black. A few were a lovely mauve.

Past tense, throughout. When the Japanese were sent home at the end of the war, this extremely profitable industry went with them.

৵

Turtles grow to great size in the southern waters. Occasionally hunters find a turtle as heavy as a horse, five hundred pounds. Turtles frequently sleep afloat a foot or two beneath the surface of the sea like slightly submerged islands. If a canoe approaches without the least sound of voice or paddle, the turtle may be speared before it wakes. Of course great care is taken to send the spear through the fleshy shoulder, not through the valuable shell.

The tortoiseshell industry depends principally upon the great hawksbill turtle of the South Seas. The animal's shell is made up of sections known technically as "deep belly," "light belly," "brown mottled shell," "brown shell," "black shell," and "yellow hoof." The last-named, a beautiful translucent yellow or cream shade, is the most valuable. Skilled artisans make beautiful tortoiseshell articles ranging from buffets, tables, vases, and jewelry boxes down to combs, hair ornaments, and cuff links.

But the artisans now get their raw material from other regions of the South Pacific. The Micronesian turtle is safe.

℘

In contrast with the beautiful turtle is the repulsive bêche-de-mer, or sea slug, a most valuable pre-war product of warm waters. This animate ooze is like a great snail, a yard long at its best, and four or five inches thick. We scooped one from the shallow sea bottom, put it on the slatted floor of the canoe, and forgot it. We looked half an hour later to see a pond of slime on the floor. In the midst of it the sea pudding, as it is well called, had mushed down through all the cracks between the slats so that there was about as much slug below the floor as above it. To separate floor and slug by force was impossible. We solved the problem only by removing the floorboard and suspending it upside down in the water. The slug gradually relaxed its hold and sank once more to the bottom—where we severely left it.

When the bêche-de-mer is cured, it shrinks from a yard in length to a foot. It is sent to China. Before use, it is placed in a chemical which restores it to its original length. It is sliced, cooked, and eaten with great relish by the Chinese. Hong Kong, Formosa, and the Chinese communities of the Philippines and Southeast Asia would take all the bêche-de-mer the Trust could supply

℘

Sharking is an exciting sport, and a profitable vocation. The South Sea islanders have always indulged in it to some extent, dangerously hunting this demon of the deep by canoe. For them it was a pastime, not a business.

Sharking on a large scale came in with the Japanese. Instead of canoes they used motor-driven schooners.

Six lines on each side of the ship passed through floating boards so arranged that the first tug would turn the white upper side of the board down and the black side up. Then the watchman blew his whistle. The men rushed to the line and pulled in the fish to the strains of a chantey. The line passed through a block in the rigging. The fish was drawn up to the block and dangled above the deck, its tremendous tail thrashing about to the peril of anyone who came near.

The official executioner, perched in the rigging, thrust a spear into the shark's forehead. Those on deck cut open the stomach, spilling the blood and viscera on the deck to the accompaniment of a terrific stench. When the shark was dead it was dropped to the deck. Many of the carcasses would list the ship, for a shark may weigh from four hundred pounds to a ton.

Jon Makoelun, splendid old native of Kusaie, sailed for nearly thirty years on the Japanese sharking ships.

"The best time was at night," he says, "especially between seven and nine o'clock. We sometimes took aboard 150 sharks during those two hours.

"We used a manila line as big as your thumb and about five fathoms long. A very long line was not necessary; the sharks chase you, you don't need to chase them. The line ended in a length of wire cable and a big hook a foot long and four inches across the bend. The best bait was a piece of pork. It took about three men, with the help of block and tackle, to haul one fish aboard.

"The five fins were cut off, dried, shipped in bags. Also we took out the liver. We squeezed it to break up the tissues, then put it in a strainer with a barrel below. The sun shining on it caused the oil in it to drain out into the barrel. It had to be kept draining for two weeks. It smelled to high heaven. So did the sharks' carcasses until we could take them ashore on the nearest island and bury them. You'd be surprised how they made the coconut trees grow."

The fins went to China as table delicacies, or for use in making gelatin. Shark oil has excellent lubricating qualities and does not get gummy, but it does have a slight odor. Much of it went to San Francisco; thence into the interior workings of sewing machines, bicycles, watches, and fine machinery. Shark-skin was used to make shoes and bags. Because the skin was covered with small, pointed, calcified papillae, cabinetmakers used it under the name of "shagreen" for smoothing and polishing wood.

The demand for these products is still there, and the shark is still there. But shark and demand no longer meet.

If these many products of land and sea were fully exploited, all would still be vanity. For they would be harvested only to rot in island warehouses, waiting for ships to transport them to world markets. In 1964 the Trust proudly announced that the addition of a new vessel, *Pacific Islander,* had raised the Trust fleet to a total of eight ships.

Eight ships to serve two thousand islands!

A main island may be visited once a month; an out island, once in six months or a year. The islander wonders why he should labor to produce more than he can eat today when tomorrow is so long in coming.

In too many cases he cannot even get his produce to the dock. On a great island such as Ponape many long miles may separate the mountain farm from the port town. Roads that once existed are now impassable, except on foot.

"The high point of the island road system," reports the investigating committee of the Pacific Science Board, "was reached in the Japanese period when community labor put in regular work on road maintenance and the Japanese military commandeered further island labor (with nominal pay) for construction of new roads for military purposes. During the Japanese period many of the high islanders owned bicycles and the roads and paths were in good enough condition so that bicycles could effect great savings of time.

"While these roads and paths were a convenience to the islanders as well as to the Japanese, they required much manual labor to maintain. Without the combined incentives of pay and threat of jail held out by the Japanese, the islanders have not in general considered that the gain was worth the effort needed to maintain the road systems. . . . In most places motor vehicle roads have reverted to footpaths and the smooth coral gravel covering on the bicycle paths has been washed away and not replaced."

Harsh compulsion, threat of jail, and only nominal pay are not recommended procedures. The only alternative is fair pay that will attract workers, but fair pay means an adequate budget and that does not exist.

Not only the natives but the administrators are severely handicapped by lack of transport. This is true not only in country districts, but within town limits. A new arrival on Truk, jolting up to the swank residential district on Nob Hill, wrote in her diary, "No road could be worse."

Later, transferred to Palau, she had this to say: "I had thought the roads on Truk were bad but that was before I rode on those in the town of Koror. They were so bumpy that you almost had to hold your stomach to keep it in place, and no one could travel more than ten miles an hour."

It is small wonder that few staff members have cared to bring their own cars to the islands. The rubble roads together

with the salt air quickly ruin any motor vehicle. One staff executive has frankly acknowledged in print, "In road building and
maintenance, we have never equaled the Japanese." And he
added bitterly, "We should bow our heads at the inadequacies
of the transportation setup."

The few repair shops are jammed to the walls and overflow
the yards with wrecked cars. The expense of buying new parts
and the long delay in getting them would suggest that it might
be cheaper to repair the roads than to repair the cars.

A cynical visitor has speculated that streets in town have
been purposely kept frightful to harmonize with the frightful
buildings. A clean, smooth pavement would contrast too violently with the rusty tin monstrosities which were thrown up
by the Navy as temporary buildings to last three years, but
which are now going on twenty. Unsightly buildings do not
inspire sightly landscaping, therefore the surroundings are har-
moniously dirty, unsanitary, and ragged, grass is uncut, weeds
flourish, and the general effect is of slipshod untidiness that
would not be tolerated around any state capital in the continental United States.

That good architecture *is* possible, even in this world of
sheet-iron horrors, is proved by some of the missions which
have erected beautiful churches and handsome schools, com-
bining cement blocks and native designs, and the remaining
Japanese government buildings such as the Palau Telephone
Exchange already mentioned and the former Japanese administration building in Palau now used as a courthouse and so fine
a piece of architecture that it is locally dubbed the Taj Mahal.

Lest I be thought just a fault-finding crank, let me call in
again Associate Chief Justice Toomin, whom I quote rather
than many other protesting staff members because as a high

executive and a judge his word should have unusual weight. In his memoirs, *Black Robe and Grass Skirt,* he refers to the Trust public buildings as "deeply humiliating to staff members who serve in the districts." Here is a showcase for visiting missions from the United Nations. "It shows the United States in the role of a miser, too penurious to pay adequately for his assumed obligations. . . . The psychologically depressing effect of working in substandard structures is manifest in a downgrading of the nature of the service by staff members, and in occasional snide comments made by the perceptive natives, many of whom remember the beautiful public buildings, shrines and torii gates erected by our predecessors the Japanese and destroyed during the bombardment."

And *New York Times* correspondent Trumbull in his report, *Paradise in Trust,* after deploring the American mess, concluded: "The only extenuation I could bring to mind for the indecent neglect everywhere in the civilian-administered areas was the frugality of the budget allotted to the Trust Territory by Congress."

In all fairness, I feel there is one other extenuation that should be kept in mind. There is good reason why the Japanese economy in the islands should have been vastly superior to our own. The Japanese were developing the islands, not for the Micronesians, but for themselves. Japan did not take the League of Nations seriously. She paid lip service to the League, but as a matter of fact she regarded the islands as an integral part of the Japanese Empire. Since the islands were at her very doorstep she naturally thought of them as a prospective home for some of her surplus population. She sent 100,000 Japanese settlers into the islands, completely overwhelming the native population of about forty thousand. She carried on large and costly projects designed to employ her own people and produce revenue for Japan. Far outnumbering the natives, the energetic

and enterprising Japanese outstripped the more leisurely islanders and occupied all important posts. The welfare of the
Micronesians was not disregarded, but it was secondary. With
us, it is primary.

The war over, all Japanese colonists were sent home. American migration to the islands was not allowed. American in-
dustrialists and businessmen were not invited. The theory was
that all private enterprises should be owned by the Micronesians.
The objective of the government was to develop Micronesian
ability and responsibility. Therefore even the president and every member of the board of directors of a company were Micronesian. They might, if they chose, hire an American manager,
but they might also fire him.

Since the tempo of island life was not that of Japan nor of
America, business projects did not grow rapidly. Some did
come into being, and they belonged to the people. The same
was true of government posts. As rapidly as seemed feasible
American officials were and are being replaced by Micronesians.

Foreigners, and that includes Americans, cannot buy land in
Micronesia. The land belongs to the Micronesians and must
remain theirs, whether they like it or not. The government has
no land to sell because it owns none. The United States does
not own an acre of Micronesian soil but acts only as the steward
of the United Nations on behalf of the island population.

The Japanese built for the centuries. We built for temporary
occupation. The agricultural director who said certain islands
would be ready for cultivation in one hundred years represented the long-term Japanese view. We hope to train the Micronesians to take care of themselves, then get out.

Japanese adventurers, invading the islands in search of easy
money, milked the natives dry for their own benefit. There was
no place in the new economy for the brown man, except as a
wage slave. And Japan even sent in wage slaves of her own to

replace him. All industries were in the hands of the Japanese. A native so unwisely enterprising as to start a shop or factory would soon find difficulty in getting supplies or machinery. His shipments would be unaccountably damaged in transit. When affairs had reached a desperate stage, a Japanese businessman would appear with an offer to buy his outfit for perhaps a tenth of what it was worth. If he was prudent, he would sell. If he stood on his "rights," his place might be destroyed some night by thugs or a fire.

Now, Micronesian enterprise is strongly encouraged. The policy of keeping all business in the hands of Micronesians has not worked perfectly and the policy has been modified so as to admit American firms but with the proviso that they must bring Micronesians into posts of responsibility as rapidly as possible.

These considerations may explain our neglect, but do not excuse it.

The real excuse, though a lame one, is confusion. The only American citizens who are not confused about the islands are those who know nothing about them. Those who do know that they exist are unclear as to their status.

They are a sort of never-never land. They are ours and not ours. They belong to the United Nations, or do they? Are they part of the United States, or a foreign land?

They are administered by the Department of the Interior, yet they are as far exterior as any land could be. Are they inside or outside? Domestic agencies of the national government won't touch them because they are outside. They don't qualify for foreign aid because they are inside. The Peace Corps, busy in a hundred foreign lands, cannot work in this territory because it is not foreign. The Federal Communications Commission is not concerned with it because it *is* foreign. The Voice of America skips it because it is domestic. The Department of the Interior gives it scant attention, being already overburdened by its duties in the million square miles of federal lands, national forests, Indian reservations. The Department of Health, Education and Welfare regards it as outside its province. Heavy customs duties are charged against it because it is foreign. Visiting commissions from the United Nations roundly criticize us for behaving as if the territory were our own property to do with as we please.

The territory is an orphan, with an indifferent and preoccupied guardian. It is a forgotten castaway in a bureaucratic limbo. An American missionary in the islands complained bitterly to a *Post* correspondent:

"Sometimes out here I've been ashamed to be an American. All we've done is maintain services for the Americans who administer the place—which is little help to the Micronesians. These people didn't ask for us; we asked for them. If we are going to keep these islands, the least we must do is pay a decent rent."

21.

Independence?

THE earth has turned on its axis since America took the Pacific islands twenty years ago. No one then could have believed there would be so radical a revolution in so short a time. Now nearly all the world's colonies have become sovereign nations.

If this miracle had been foreseen, it is doubtful that America would have assumed the overlordship of Micronesia. She would not have welcomed the prospect of being left out on a limb with the last of the colonialists.

America never really wanted the islands. She did not want war with Japan. It was precipitated by Pearl Harbor. At the war's end, the islands were in American hands.

What to do? They could not be given back to Japan as possible stepping-stones for another Japanese imperialistic adventure sometime in the future. Nor did America relish the idea of having them pass into the hands of some other world power.

She kept them to prevent anyone else from taking them. Still green was the memory of what had happened at the close of the Spanish-American War. At that time these very islands were American spoils of war. America regarded them as an unwelcome burden and passed them back to Spain. Spain's fangs had been pulled; surely her possession of the islands would constitute no threat to anyone.

But Spain unexpectedly sold the islands to Germany, the last power on earth America could desire as a neighbor in the Pacific.

Nothing of this sort should be allowed to happen again. So America kept control of the islands, but sought to avert criticism by going through the formality of accepting them as a "trust territory" of the United Nations. The globe was still profusely spotted with colonies, so a colony under the disarming title of Trust Territory would hardly attract notice.

But practically all the colonies have now vanished. The trust territories, once numerous, have now been reduced to three: Micronesia under the United States, New Guinea and Nauru under Australia.

America and Australia stand naked in the storm. Australia smarts under verbal attacks by her Asiatic neighbors, by most African states, and by all Communist governments; and by attacks worse than verbal over the border that uncertainly separates her portion of New Guinea from the western part which its confiscator, Indonesia, calls West Irian. These border raids can be expected to increase in volume and virulence. It is the fully acknowledged ambition of Indonesia to incorporate all of the great island of New Guinea, second largest in the world, in the Empire of Indonesia.

This may be a fairly easy matter, once Australian protection has been withdrawn. The territory has no means of self-defense. Pre-emption of the entire island would bring Indonesia within a few dozen miles of Australia itself. Much too close for comfort.

And yet, as I learned from interviews with the chief guardians of the Trust, Australia fully expects that New Guinea must be given independence within ten years.

Many steady-minded New Guineans don't want Australian authority to end so soon, believing the people not yet trained in democracy, and quite conscious of what too-hasty independence has done to the Congo. But the thoughtless ones and those who seek personal power are for "freedom."

Chief pressure comes from the United Nations whose many Afro-Asian members know nothing about New Guinea, except that Australia has it. A UN visiting commission comes every three years and while some of its members (such as the Indians) have had enough experience with colonial conditions to see good in Australia's administration, more radical and less knowledgeable members, especially those with Communist leanings, are critical. And of course there's always something to criticize, even in the best administration.

As for Nauru, the inhabitants of this small equatorial island are embroiled in a bitter dispute with the administering country and demand immediate independence.

It seems almost a certainty that Australia will shake off both burdens in the near future and America will be left to face the music alone.

America cannot quit now. With her hand in the bottle and full of islands she cannot easily get it out. She has assumed responsibilities which she has not yet fulfilled. And, if she left, the islands would immediately be taken over by some new landlord. Who would that be?

Japan would be an immediate and urgent applicant. Russia looks out on the Pacific and once reached across it to grasp Alaska and what is now British Columbia. She would conceivably be interested once more in a chance to extend her power at least halfway across the Pacific. Red China also flanks this ocean and could ask for nothing better than a shield of two thousand islands behind which she could carry on her program for the enslavement of Southeast Asia.

Fully as scornful of "peaceful coexistence" is Indonesia. We carelessly think of Indonesia as a fairly harmless group of tropical islands controlled by a petty tyrant more capable of bluster than of blood. But Indonesia, though narrow, sprawls across the southern ocean for thirty-five hundred miles, a thousand miles more than the span of continental United States. With West New Guinea now tucked under its belt, Indonesia repeatedly discusses in its press and official documents the possibility of adding the island group immediately north of New Guinea. That is Micronesia. The fact that the people of the two nesias are not the same would not trouble Indonesia which already governs such diverse races as the Bataks, Malays, Chinese, Dyaks, and Papuans.

❦

The strategic importance of the Micronesian sea, the world's largest colonial area, can hardly be overestimated.

Micronesia sparked World War II in the Pacific. Without it, even the hotheads of Japan would not have dreamed of making war on the United States. Micronesia was, in the words of a Japanese admiral, "the key to the Pacific." A glance at the map shows why. Micronesia dominates the entire western Pacific from Japan to the equator and from the Philippines to Hawaii.

From bases in these islands it was only a one-hour flight to Pearl Harbor, one hour to Luzon, one hour to Tarawa in the Gilberts, two hours or less to any of the great prizes of the south, New Guinea, the Bismarcks, New Britain, the Solomon Islands, and Australia itself.

Three months before Pearl Harbor this writer was talking with a young Australian about his country's fear of Japan.

"I think it's foolish," he said. "Why should we be afraid of Japan? Japan is thousands of miles from Australia."

"I think you are mistaken," I said. "Japan is closer to Australia than I am to you."

He smiled at what he took for an effort to be facetious.

"I'll go further than that," I added. "The Japanese world and the Australian world are as close together as the drops in that glass of water."

I spread out a map, not the sort that appears in a school geography, but a navigation chart worked out in great detail. I showed him the Australian islands extending to the equator. He knew about them, but was puzzled by the swarm of islands north of the equator.

"What are they?" he asked. "Most maps don't show them."

They bore such names as the Carolines, Marshalls, Marianas, and over the mass of them was lettered MICRONESIA—JAPANESE MANDATE.

The southern limit of the Japanese Mandate was shown to be the equator—and the northern limit of the Australian Mandate was also the equator. Along that line, for some fourteen hundred miles, Australian and Japanese sovereignty met.

The young Australian pored over the island labyrinth with growing excitement.

"Why," he said, "they are in the middle of everything, aren't they? Close to Hawaii, just a jump from Japan, slap up against Australian waters, right next to the Dutch Indies—and look at the Philippines, smothered by them!"

The Pearl Harbor attack, December 7, 1941, was launched from the Marshalls and was almost immediately followed by a push from the Carolines to the west, the south, the east, and even the north. Before the end of the month Guam, Wake, the Gilberts, and the Philippines were in Japanese hands. Before August of 1942 the Japanese had swarmed ashore on the islands of Indonesia, New Guinea, the Bismarcks, and the Solomons. Japan was firmly planted in the island possessions of Australia.

The dream had been bigger than that. It had included Australia itself, a continent seventeen times the size of Japan and with one-twelfth the population. The Japanese were intensely interested in the theory of redistribution of territory, once suggested by Colonel House and endorsed in principle by Sir Samuel Hoare. If the "have" nations were to share their open spaces with the "have not" nations, the Japanese could think of no better place to begin than in Australia. Fortunately by this time the Allied military had caught its breath and Australia was saved.

It may be argued that with the dawn of the nuclear age island bases are no longer important. Military strategists do not endorse this comfortable theory. It may become technically possible to fire a missile from the California coast to Asia, but only at staggering expense, and considerable uncertainty of pinpointing the target. Hawaii is closer but, as we have learned, Hawaii is highly vulnerable. The sea between California and Hawaii is empty. The sea between Hawaii and Asia swarms with potential bases.

The best part of an atoll is the part that has been left out of it. The lagoon is an ideal shelter for Polaris submarines and aircraft. No longer will it be safe to concentrate a great fleet in a single lagoon where it may be wiped out by a lone hydrogen bomb. The availability of two thousand islands makes such a concentration unnecessary. Dispersal into smaller units in numerous scattered harbors is the new strategy. As military commentator Hanson W. Baldwin has pointed out, small widely scattered bases present the potential enemy with a problem he cannot solve. He must attack all the island bases as well as those in North America almost simultaneously or lose the advantage of surprise. The more separate bases there are, the more insuperable is the difficulty of crushing them before heavy retaliation can take place.

So we have a curious contradiction. The islands are considered "logistically indispensable" because they serve as launching stations for our missiles and space satellites and tracking stations for those of an enemy—matters of growing importance in view of the existence of a large Soviet submarine fleet, not to mention the growing submarine force and future nuclear potential of Communist China. But at the same time we may fervently wish that we were out of the islands, free of responsibility for their inhabitants, cleared of the stigma of colonialism.

⚜

But since we are there, why not make colonialism what it has sometimes been in the past, a virtue rather than a vice? Colonialism is not bad *per se.* Many of the new nations are indebted to colonialism for their training in nationhood. Colonialism is a curse if it means neglect and exploitation.

We can hardly be charged with exploitation. We take nothing out of the islands. Our fault is that we do not put enough in—enough to keep body and soul together, enough to pay "a decent rent" for our present and potential bases.

"Here, thinks the Micronesian, is the fabled Rich American," writes James Ramsey Ullman. "He owns the world—or at least half of it. He can buy anything he wants. He thinks nothing of giving millions of dollars to any tinhorn strong man in Asia or Africa who agrees to whistle 'The Star-Spangled Banner.' But for us there is almost nothing. A dole—a handout. We make no trouble, so we are forgotten. We are the isolation ward, the poorhouse."

The islanders undoubtedly think these things but rarely say them. Much more vocal are the investigating missions from the United Nations. Their visits cause considerable trepidation in the offices of both the island administration and the Department of the Interior in Washington.

Fear of the castigating whip of the UN was expressed by Assistant Secretary of the Interior John A. Carver when he whispered to me at a Majuro cocktail party, "They're really going to get after us."

They did. The UN visiting mission of 1964 went home to report to the UN Trusteeship Council that something was seriously amiss with island education: there was a dearth of vocational and technical training, adults who needed education were not getting it, broadcasting was not developed, and the advancement of women did not keep pace with that of men. In the economic field the report suggested:

> A greater and more positive effort should be made to stimulate economic development both for its own sake and to insure that a desirable balance is attained between economic and social development programs.

At the same time the report acknowledged

> the respect and trust shown in Micronesia towards the High Commissioner, Mr. Goding. The mission heard many criticisms of policies and people, but even the severest critics were at pains to make clear that they considered Mr. Goding to be the best thing that had happened to Micronesia for many years.

Mr. Goding and his administration have inspired new hope in despairing islanders. It may be an illusory hope. Even the most enlightened administration with the best intentions in the world cannot accomplish the needed miracles in reconstruction without tools. The tools are dollars.

How do the Micronesians feel about the American presence? Have they caught the fever for independence now sweeping the world?

In Palau there is a simmering volcano of discontent. It is the more dangerous because it has religious and fanatic overtones. The native-born religion derived from the aforementioned cargo cult assures its devotees that the white man's world is about to collapse and all his treasures will be shipped to the islands, there to be freely distributed to all who have brown or black skins. At the same time all whites will leave the islands and the natives will rule themselves.

Priests of the new faith conduct elaborate white-cursing rituals and stir their listeners to a frenzy of expectation. Sentinels are posted on hilltops to watch for the treasure-bearing ships. According to a current report of the Administration the cult now embraces one third of the population of Palau and is growing.

Americans have themselves to blame, in part, for the cargo superstition. During the war the armed forces prodigally gave away everything for which they had no immediate use. Surplus food, clothing, building materials, radios, refrigerators, half-worn machines of every sort, were distributed with a lavish hand. Particularly at the war's end there was a dumping on a colossal scale, quite unparalleled in history. Then the white men boarded their ships and planes and went away.

Why couldn't it happen again, and on a bigger scale? This was the way to easy riches. Perhaps this time the white man would sail away and never come back.

Recently in some of the islands south of Palau the cargo cult has changed into the Johnson cult. How this could be is hard to conceive, but it is officially reported in New Britain, New Guinea, and the Solomons. By some mental twist which only fanaticism makes possible, the idea spread that the fleet of treasure ships was about to be sent on its way by President Johnson. Therefore he enjoys great popularity down under. In fact he has been elected. In recent New Guinea elections people who were told to vote for the one they preferred as their chief official have been voting for Johnson.

Palau, nearest Micronesian island to New Guinea, is the only Trust island seriously affected as yet by the cargo cult. Even in Palau, two thirds of the people are not fretful under American administration and in the other islands sentiment is still more favorable.

The concord between rulers and ruled impressed Sir John Macpherson, chairman of one of the visiting missions from the UN:

> The most vivid and lasting impression that we carried with us, after a month's traveling and after seeing thousands of people, was of the genuine cordiality and easiness of the relations between the Micronesians and the United States officials in the Trust Territory, and of the mutual trust and confidence that exists between them.
>
> It would perhaps be going too far to say that nothing else matters, but I suggest that, where such conditions and such an atmosphere exist, nothing can go very far wrong.

The comment is too indulgent. Something has gone pretty far wrong in the economics of the islands. Yet, in spite of diminished income and opportunity, the islanders like their white guardians because "they treat us like human beings."

Said one Trukese, "We like the Americans because they don't dictate but cooperate."

Said another, "They don't dominate us. We work together on mutual problems."

Other comments were:

"The Germans and Japanese gave orders. The Americans talk things over with us."

"The Americans don't interfere with our customs."

"But," I asked, "don't you ever think about independence?"

The reply was generally something like this: "Of course. Some day we'd like to be independent. But not now. It wouldn't work. We couldn't get along with each other—too many differences. Different languages, different customs."

Said a Marshallese: "It's a mistake to lump us all together as Micronesians. We Marshallese don't want to be classed with Ponapeans any more than France would care to merge with Germany or China with Japan."

"All we ask," said a Trukese sheriff, "is to be governed by a country that doesn't lose wars."

This is certainly a reasonable wish considering how lost wars have pushed Micronesia about from Spain to Germany to Japan to America.

℘

Not only is there very little nationalist sentiment in the islands, but many native leaders favor closer rather than looser ties with the United States. The powerful Amata Kabua, who has never hesitated to criticize American policy even on the floor of the United Nations, told me, "Independence is impractical for islands so widely scattered and so diverse in language and custom."

He would like to see the islands become a territory of the United States, like Guam. In Saipan, Chief Sablan said, "If a plebiscite were taken, ninety-nine percent of the people would vote to become a territory of the United States."

The graduation of Hawaii into statehood has started some Micronesians talking about the possibility of their islands becoming the fifty-first state.

"Micronesia would be best off as an outright U.S. possession," declares Dwight Heine of the Marshalls, a man who cannot be accused of being rabidly pro-American, since his has been the strongest voice raised on the floor of the United Nations in New York against the testing of nuclear bombs in the Pacific islands.

In Palau, home of the dissident cargo cult, two political parties fought to elect legislators in the fall of 1963. It might have been expected that one of the parties would be dedicated to the cause of independence. It was not so. The two contenders were the Liberal Party, which espoused the status quo, and the Progressive Party, which advocated closer connection with the United States under which the Trust Territory would become a member of the "American Commonwealth."

African members of UN visiting missions have tried to stir the islanders to demand complete self-determination. They have had no success. Micronesian leaders have not been fooled by that magniloquent word. They know that unbridled self-determination is impossible. If each island of a few hundred or a few thousand people were to constitute its own government, we should have a myriad of sovereign nations in the Pacific. The result, chaos and constant war.

Self-determination is an impossible and even criminal ideal. No individual may determine his conduct to suit himself; it is determined largely by the needs of others as set down in constitutions and laws. Nor has any group of people, calling itself a nation, the right to conduct itself regardless of the rights of other groups or nations.

The doctrine of self-determination has spread much false hope and bitter disillusionment in the world. It should be replaced by some such term as interdependence. Only the general good of the world may ultimately determine the behavior of the individual or the nation.

I asked many chiefs for their opinions on this score—why

should not each island or each group of islands govern itself?
Their views were pretty well summed up in the opinion of a
Ponape chief:

"When we ruled ourselves, every chief was at war with every
other. It is better to have some higher authority."

Micronesians are aware of what has been going on in Africa.
They know the troubles of new nations that have taken on the
burdens of self-rule before they were ready to bear them. There
is an uneasy suspicion, not that America may stay, but that she
may leave too soon. One of the UN missions recognized this
danger:

> Paradoxical as this may seem, the Mission is, therefore, of
> the opinion that in order to increase and hasten the construc-
> tive participation of Micronesians in the administration, it is
> essential at this stage to increase rather than decrease the
> number of American employees.

There is real danger that the United States, so sensitive to
world opinion and unhappy to be thought a colonialist power,
may step out of the islands before the people are prepared to
take over. A native official in Majuro told us:

"We're being pushed too fast. We have a few trained men—
men who could lead. But there's no second team. Nor third
team. To make a stable government you've got to have enough
good men in subordinate positions to back up the leaders. Our
people are not trained to plan ahead. They think just for today.
Just one little example out of hundreds: we import outboard
motors but don't bother to bring in spare parts at the same
time. A motor conks out and lies idle for perhaps as much as six
months waiting for the part we need to repair it."

A sense of responsibility is growing as the Administration
places more natives in important posts and they discover their
own abilities. The Japanese regime and the German gave them

no such opportunity. American officials are firmly committed to train the Micronesians for self-government, but what form that self-government may finally take is up to the Micronesians themselves.

The people of every community are encouraged to organize a municipality with a locally elected municipal council which has power, subject to checks by the Hicom, to levy taxes, supervise education, conduct public works. The local council sends its delegate to a district-wide Congress.

"You have only to attend the district Congresses," said Judge Toomin, "and listen to the delegates debate to develop a profound respect for the intelligence and capacity of many of the native leaders."

Once a year there is a top conference at Trust headquarters of all the district leaders. There problems of a territorial nature are considered and recommendations made to the Hicom.

That worthy is still the boss. His power is dictatorial if he chooses to make it so. He is both the executive branch of the government and the legislative—he makes the laws. A capricious Hicom might do considerable damage. As rapidly as possible the legislative power will be taken over by the territorial council.

As for judicial power, it is already pretty much in the hands of the people. Local magistrates are elected. All judges of district and community courts are natives. The Chief Justice and Associate Chief Justice of the Territory are Americans.

Women have equal access to courts and equal rights to own property or hold public office. Their political activity, however, is still strongly influenced by the differing customs of the various islands.

Any inhabitant of the Territory has the right of petition to the UN, and the right has frequently been exercised. The Ad-

ministration distributes each year the verbatim records of the
UN Trusteeship Council so that the people of the Territory
may understand the suggestions or criticisms of the UN. The
problems of island government bulk large in the social studies
program of every high school and there are also adult classes in
the same subject. The Micronesians of today have a pretty fair
idea of the democratic process. Outside of the cargo cult minor-
ity in Palau, no one is likely to vote for Johnson; nor, as happened in the Congo, strip naked in the voting booth under the
impression that he is to have a medical examination.

ℰ

But, when everything favorable that can be said has been
said, the fact remains that the Trust is progressing backward. A
static appropriation with rising costs inevitably means that less
and less can be done.

Harassed officials point out that the budget of the single island of Guam, a U.S. possession, has been larger than that of
the whole Trust.

Saipan when administered by the free-spending Navy enjoyed a larger budget than all the rest of the Trust put together.

Congress is not the real culprit after all. The American public is responsible. A congressman takes instructions from his
constituents. But his constituents cannot advise him in the matter, for they themselves may never have heard of Micronesia.
The average American is not aware of his country's disgrace in
the western Pacific. African, Asian, and Communist delegates to
the UN know more about it than he.

Instead of operating in semi-secrecy, the Trust should have
an active public relations department. "The main thing now,"
says Dwight Heine, "is to let America know we exist." The

facts should be released, not only the good but the bad as well. Nothing would do the Trust more good than some bad publicity. Only by a thorough dose of the bitter truth can a generous but uninformed public be alerted to its responsibility for the Forgotten Sisters of the richest nation on earth.

Index